HEROPXLS

DRAWING BOOK

4x4 PIXEL ART GRID

LARGE EDITION

4 GRIDS PER PAGE

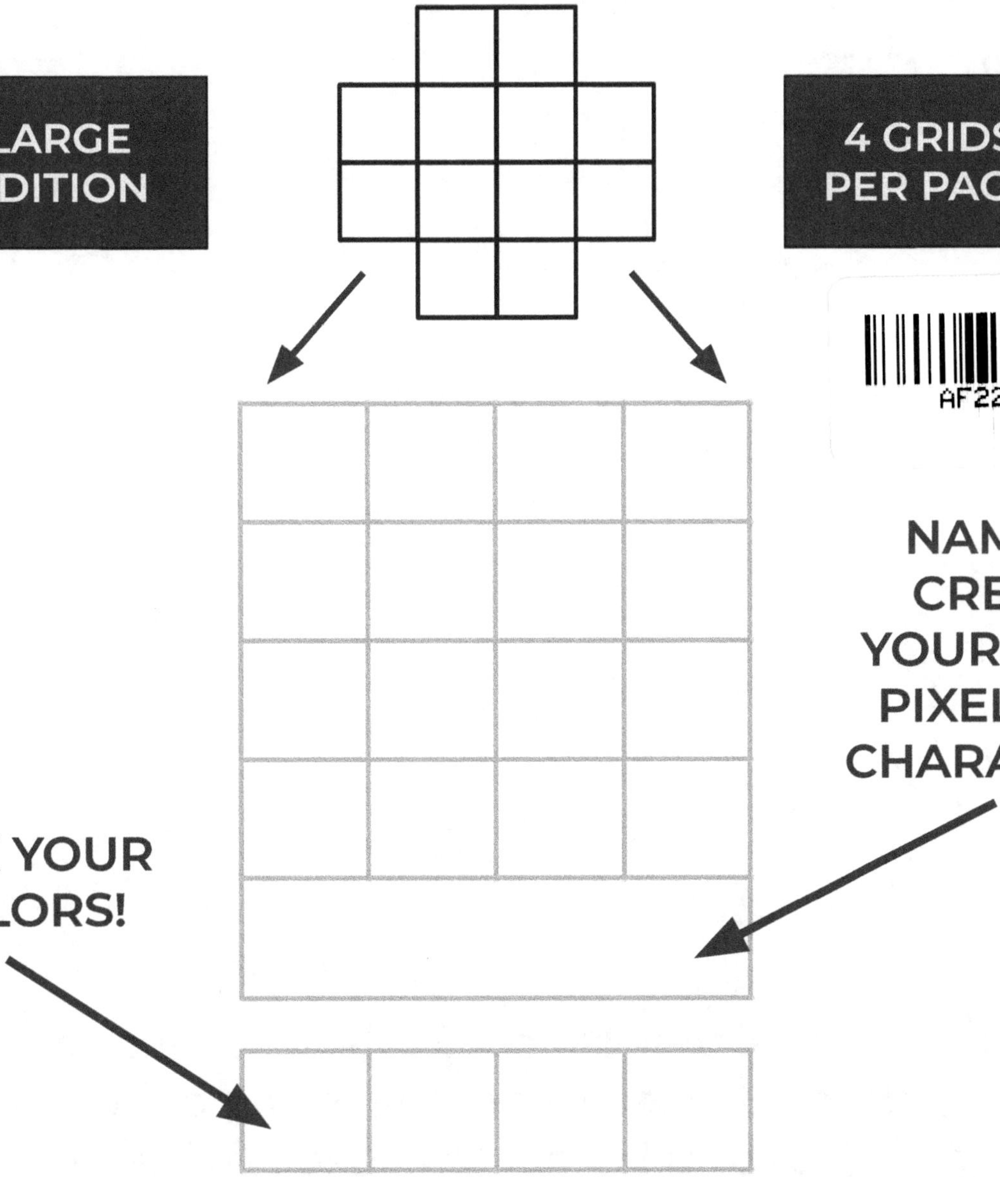

AF225237

NAME & CREATE YOUR OWN PIXEL ART CHARACTER!

PICK YOUR COLORS!

INCLUDES 200 PIXEL ART TEMPLATES

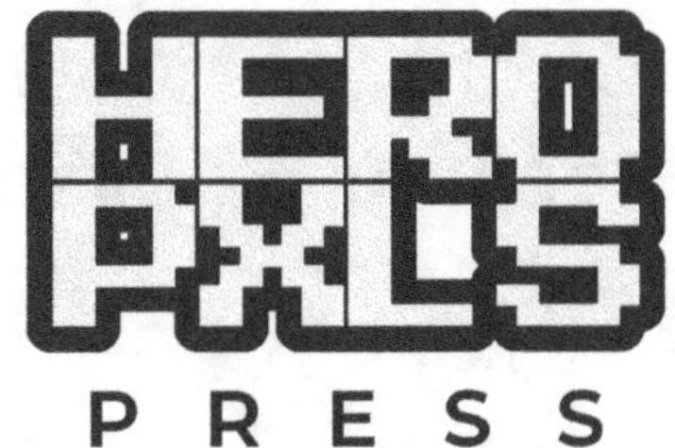

HERO PXLS

PRESS

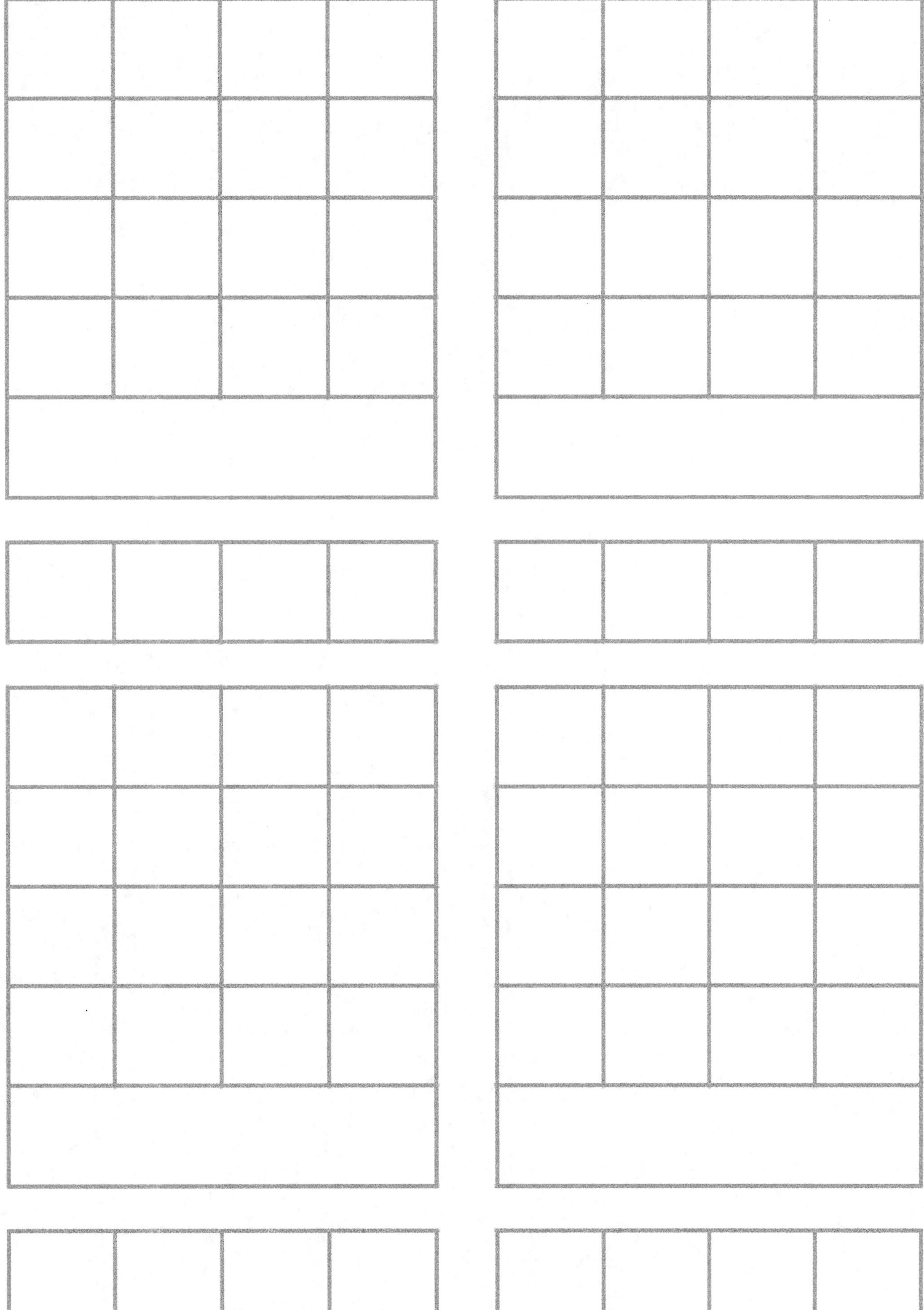

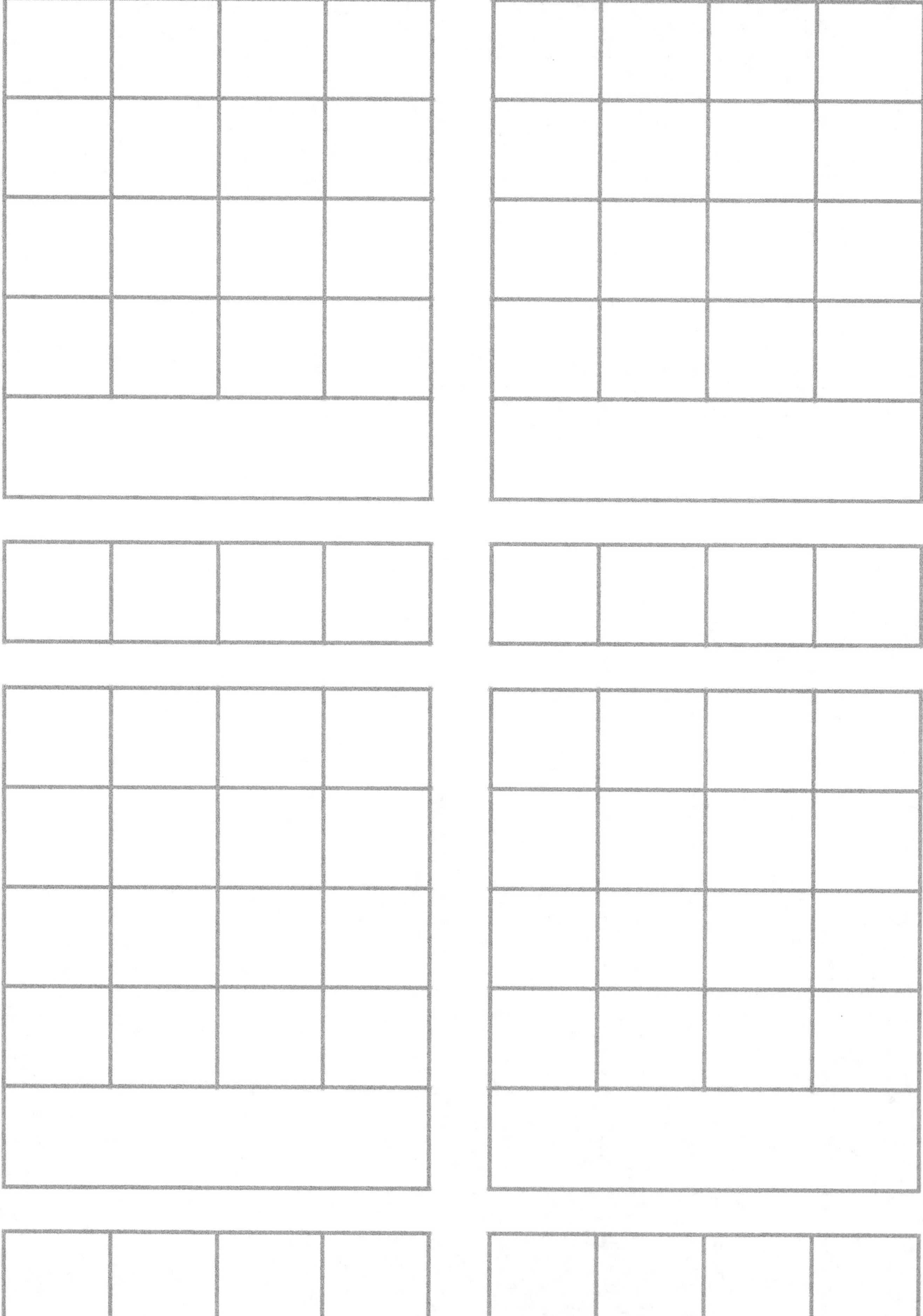

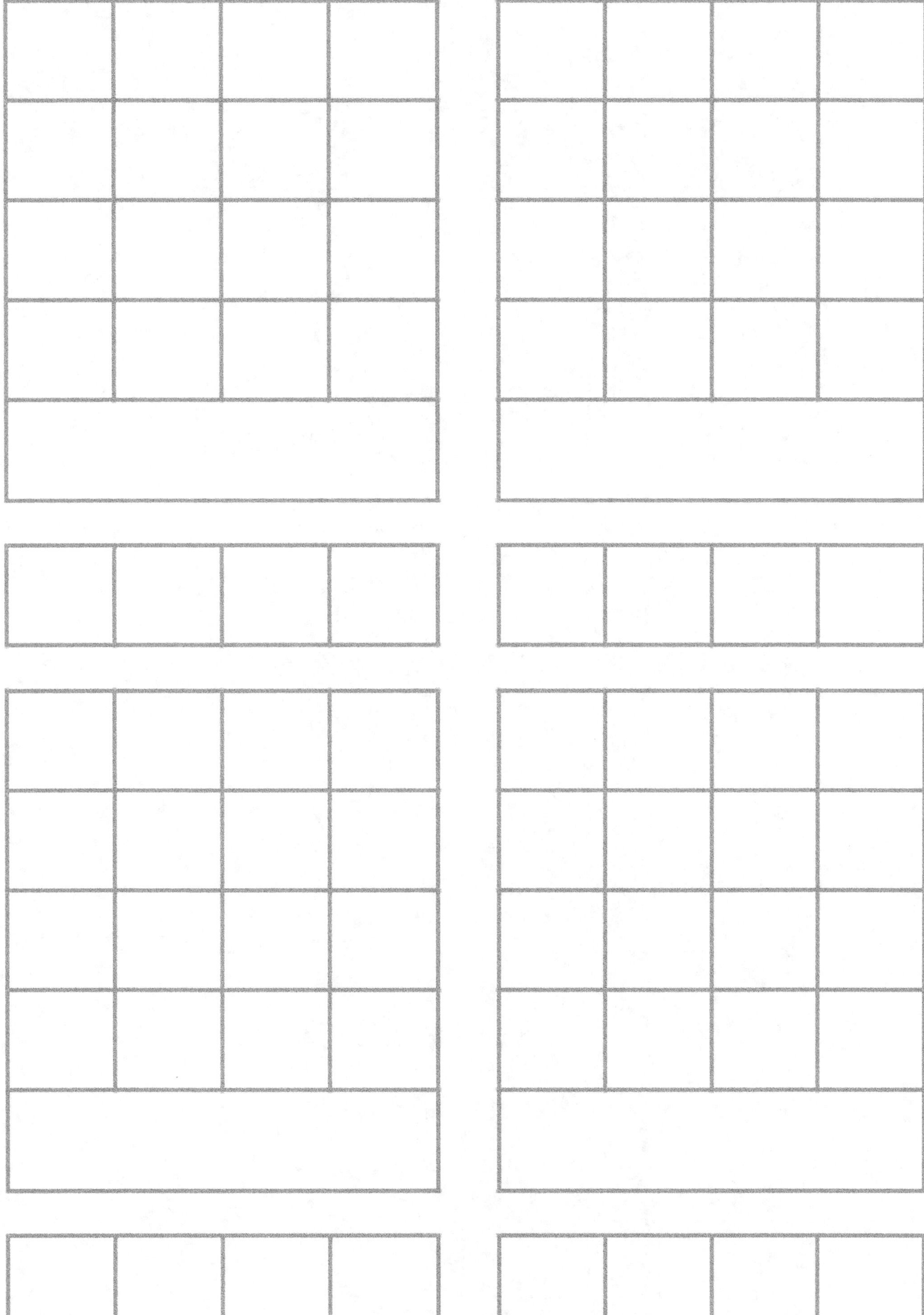

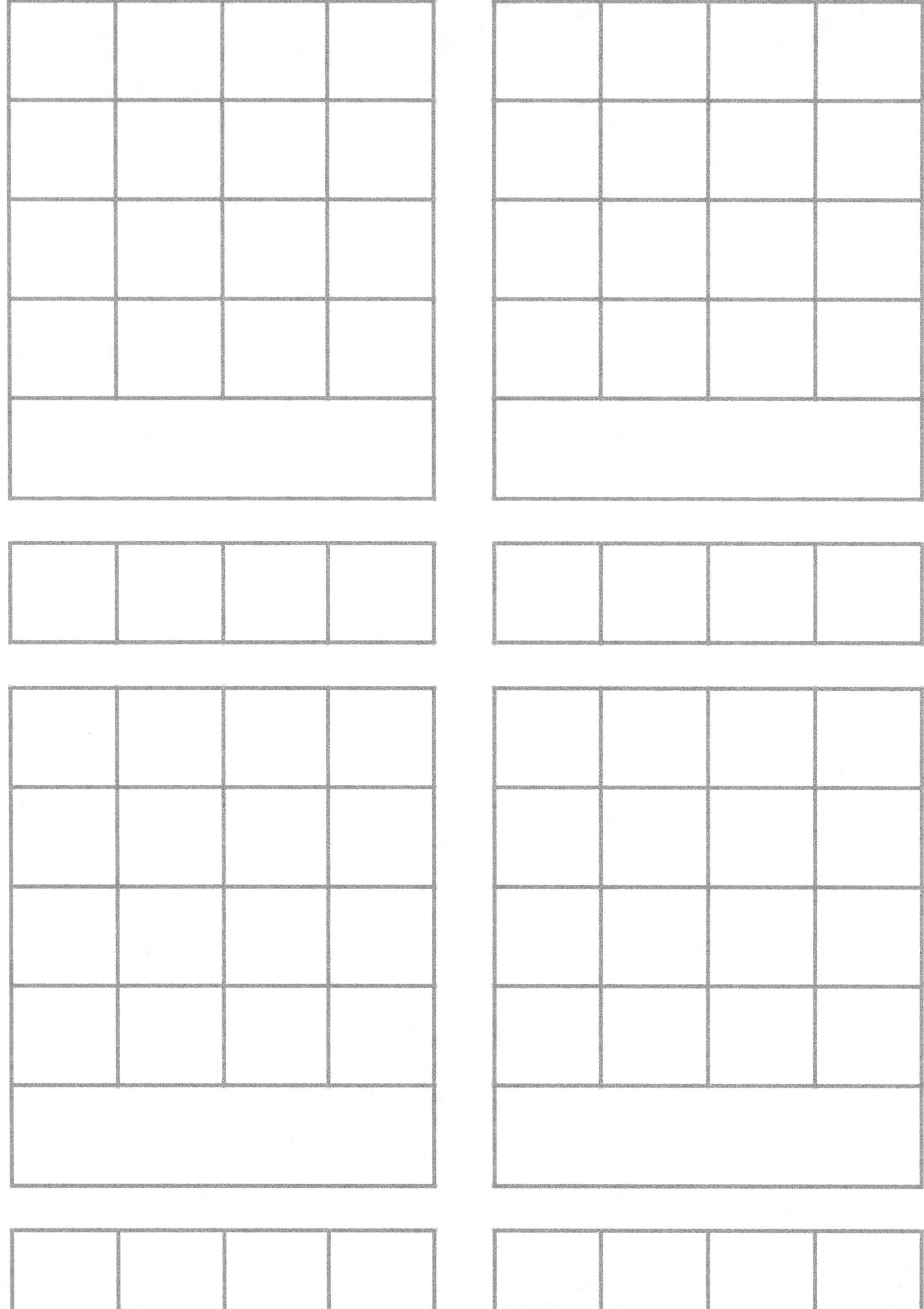

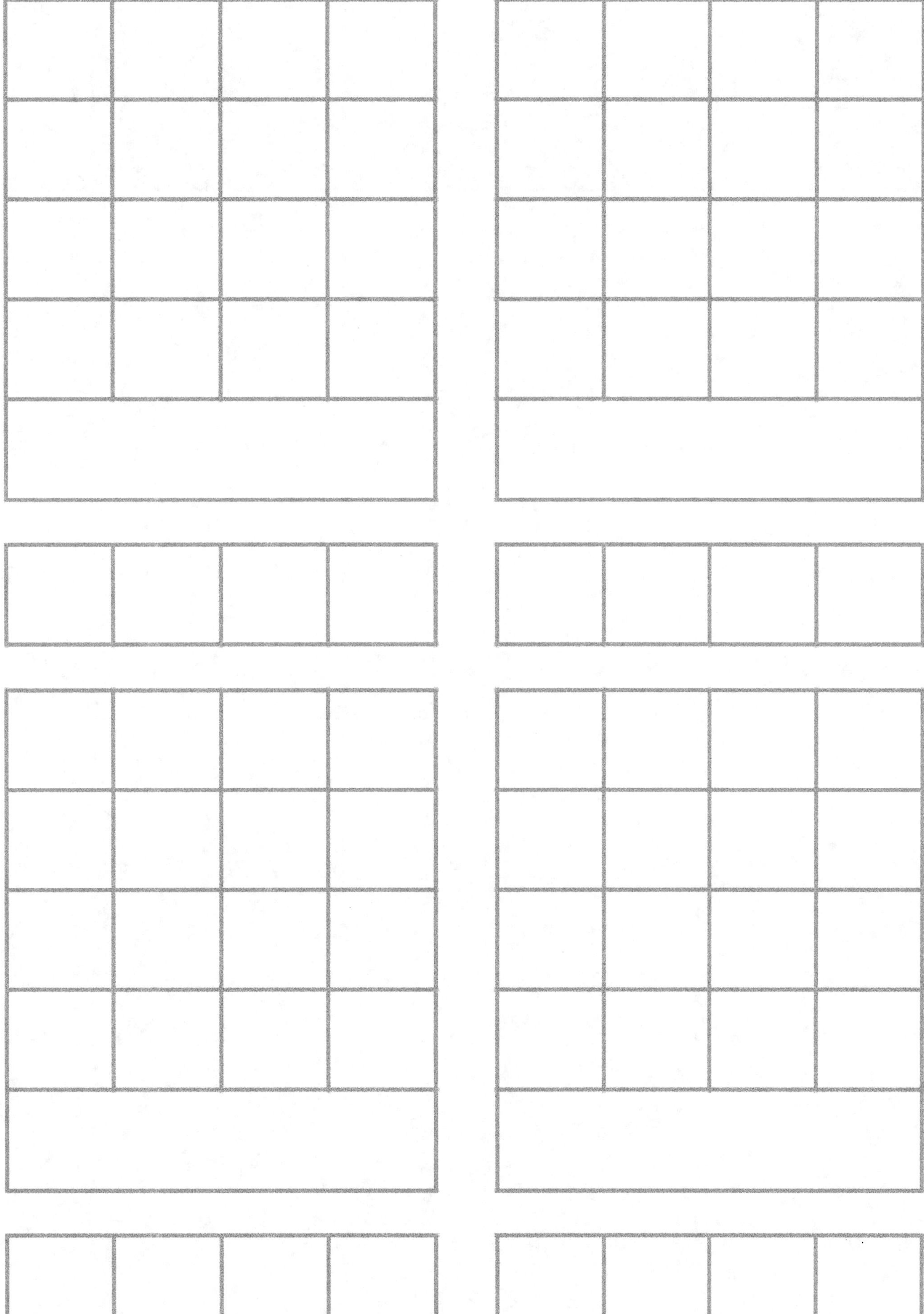

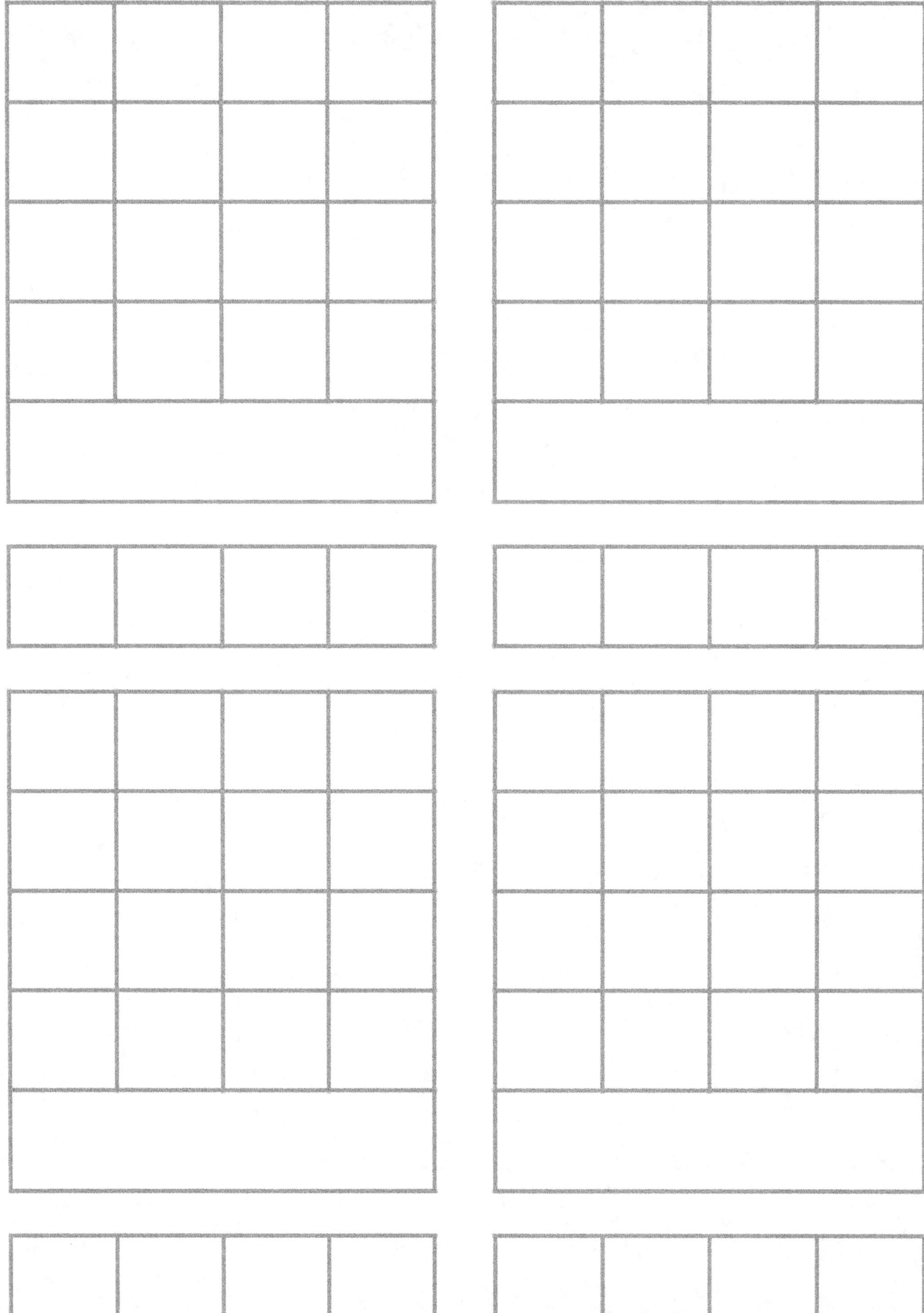

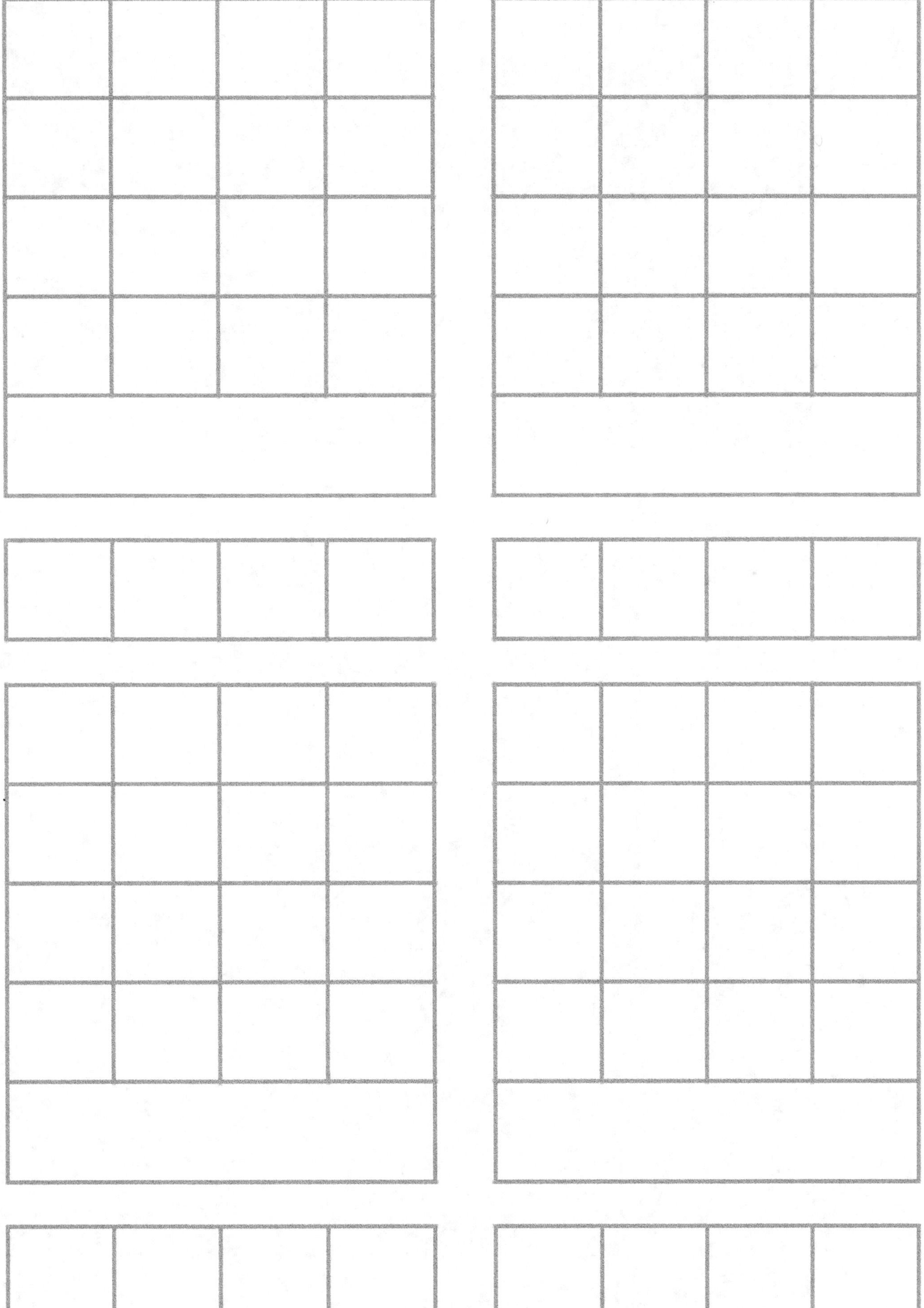

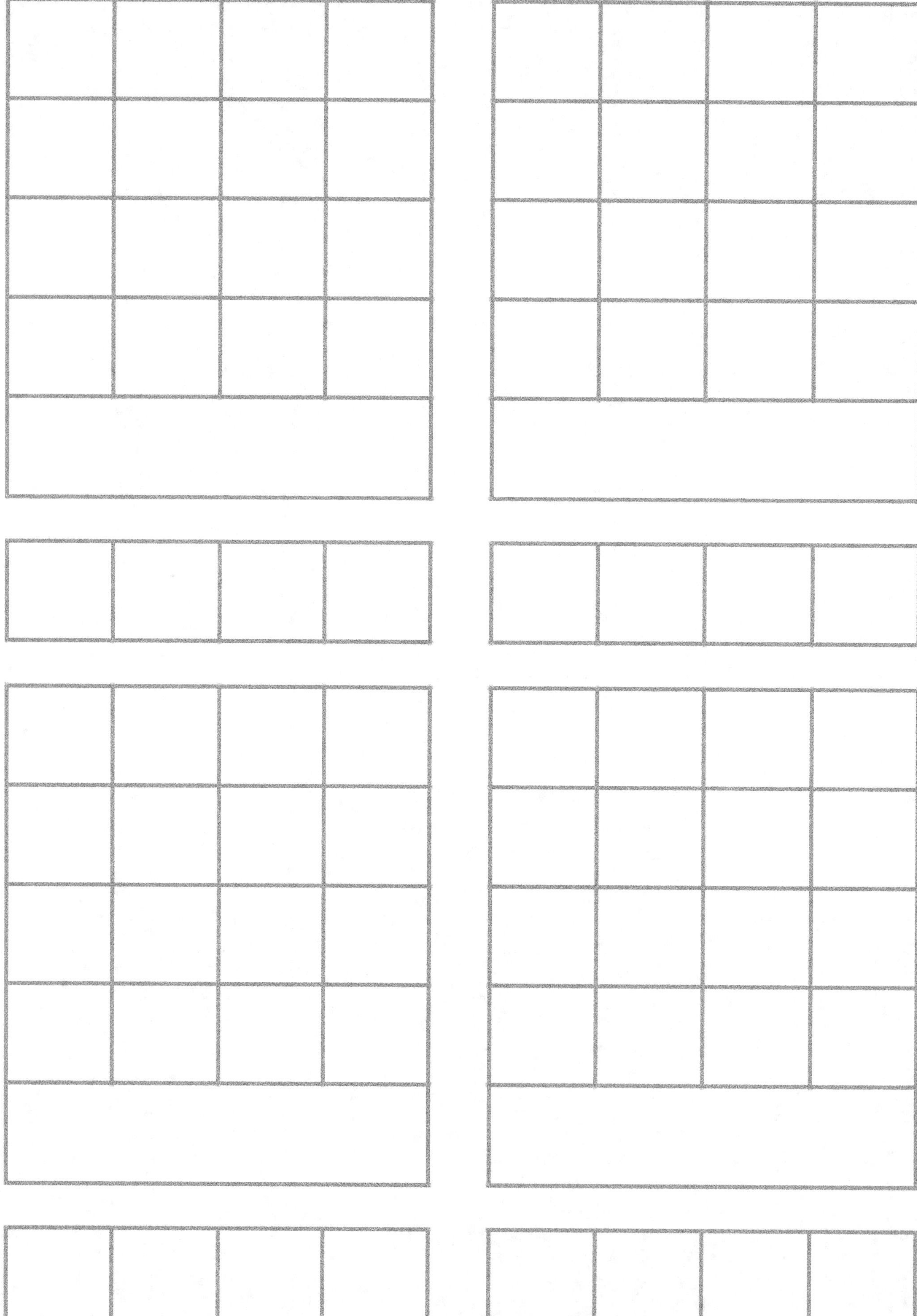

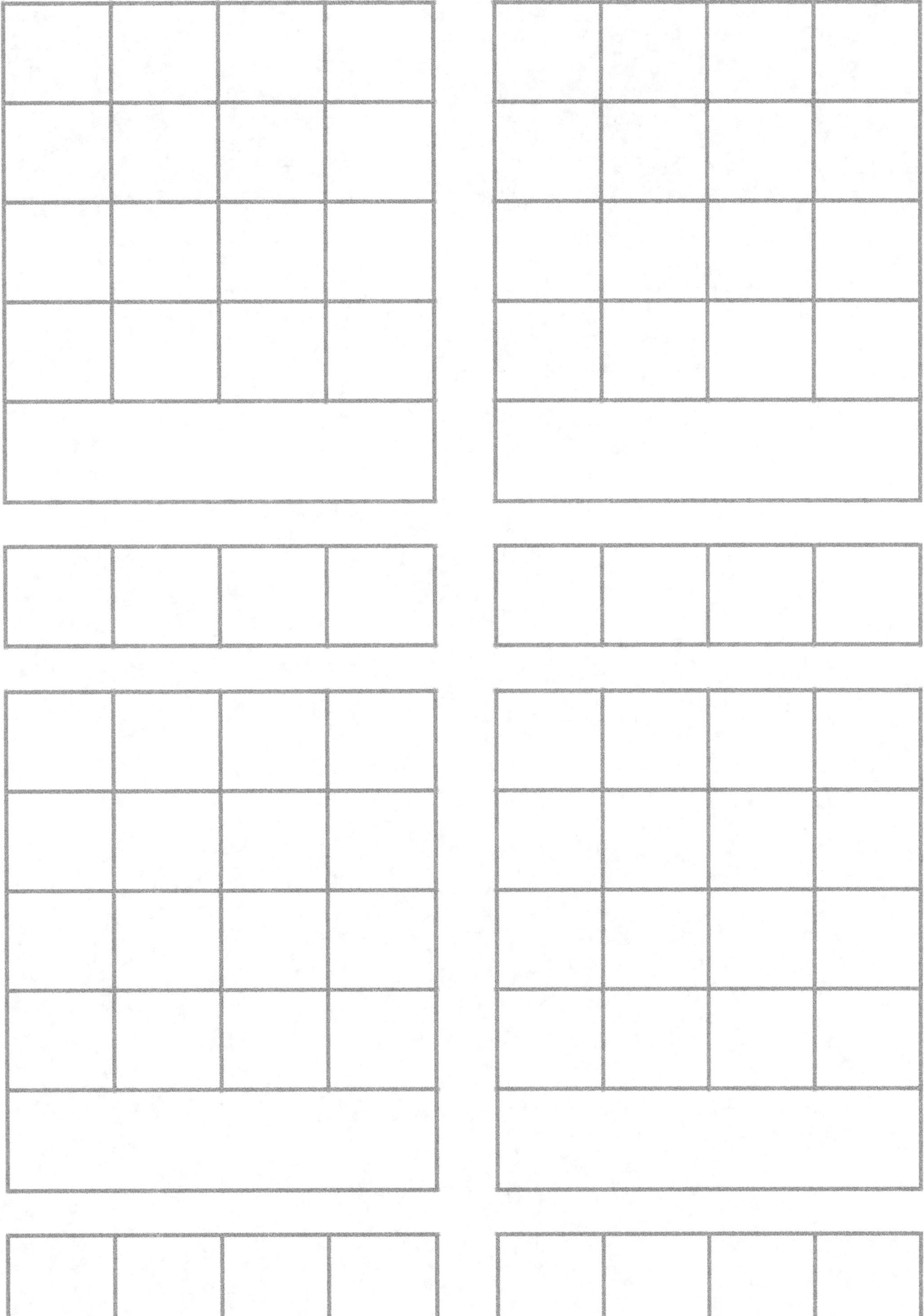

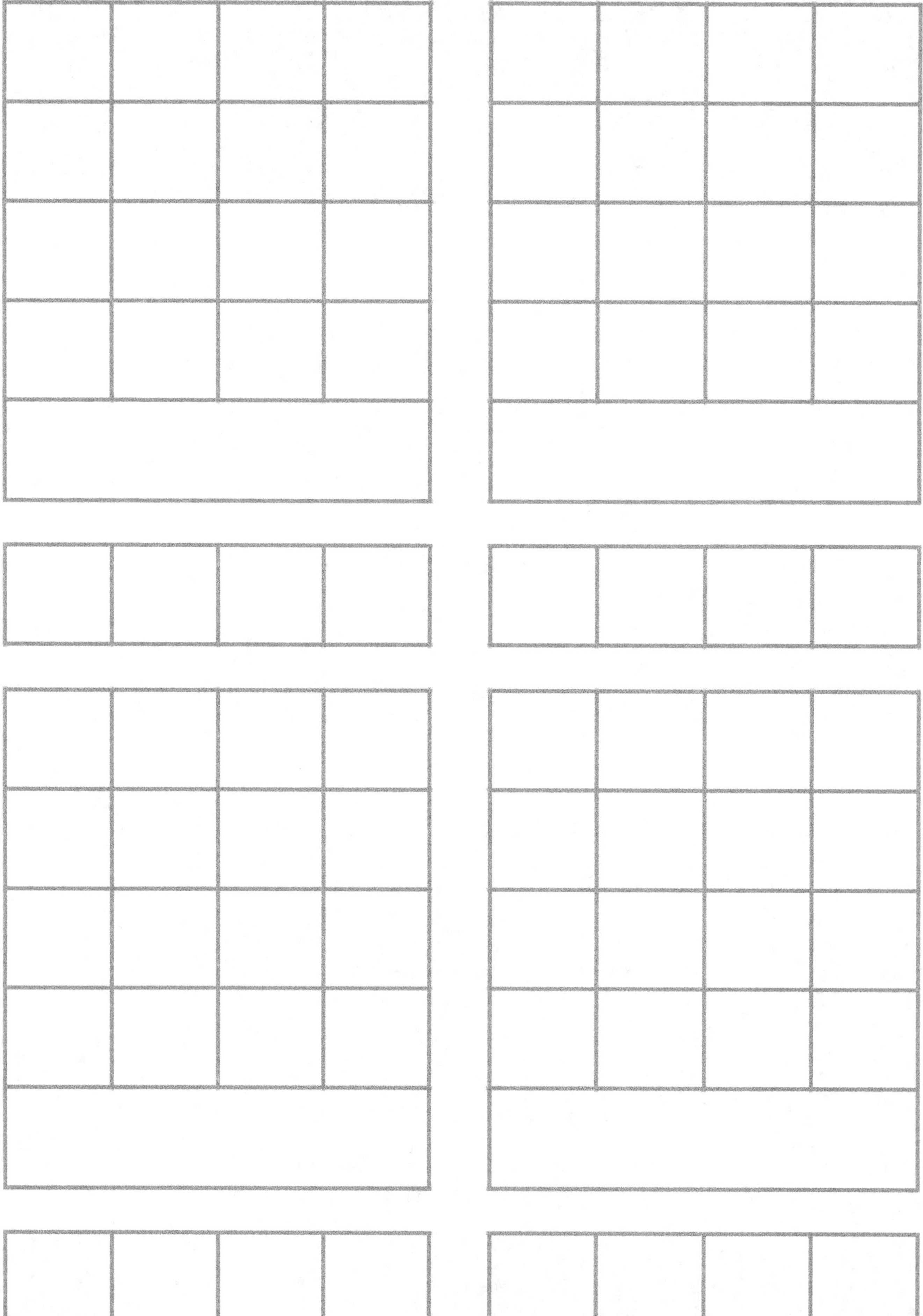

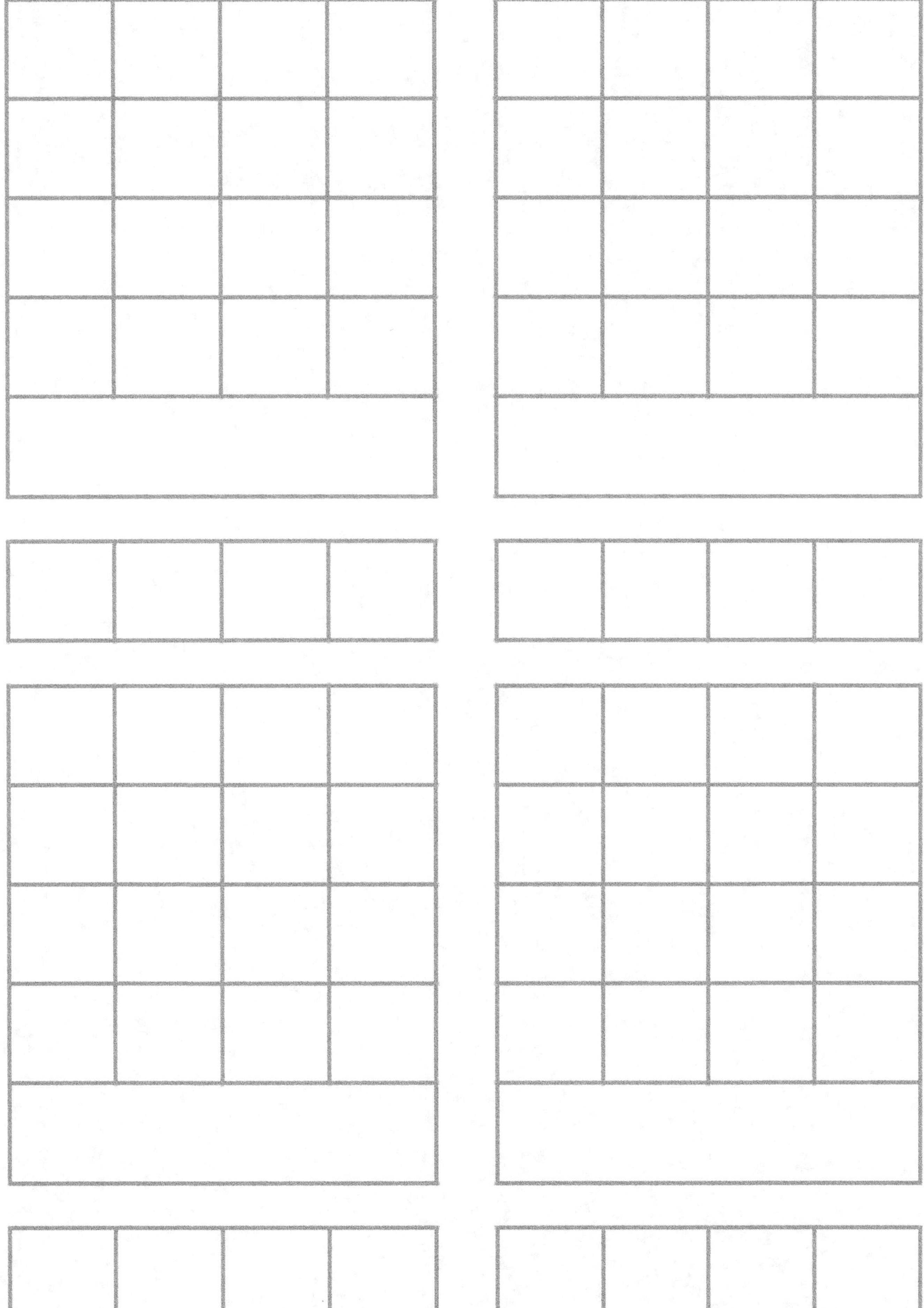

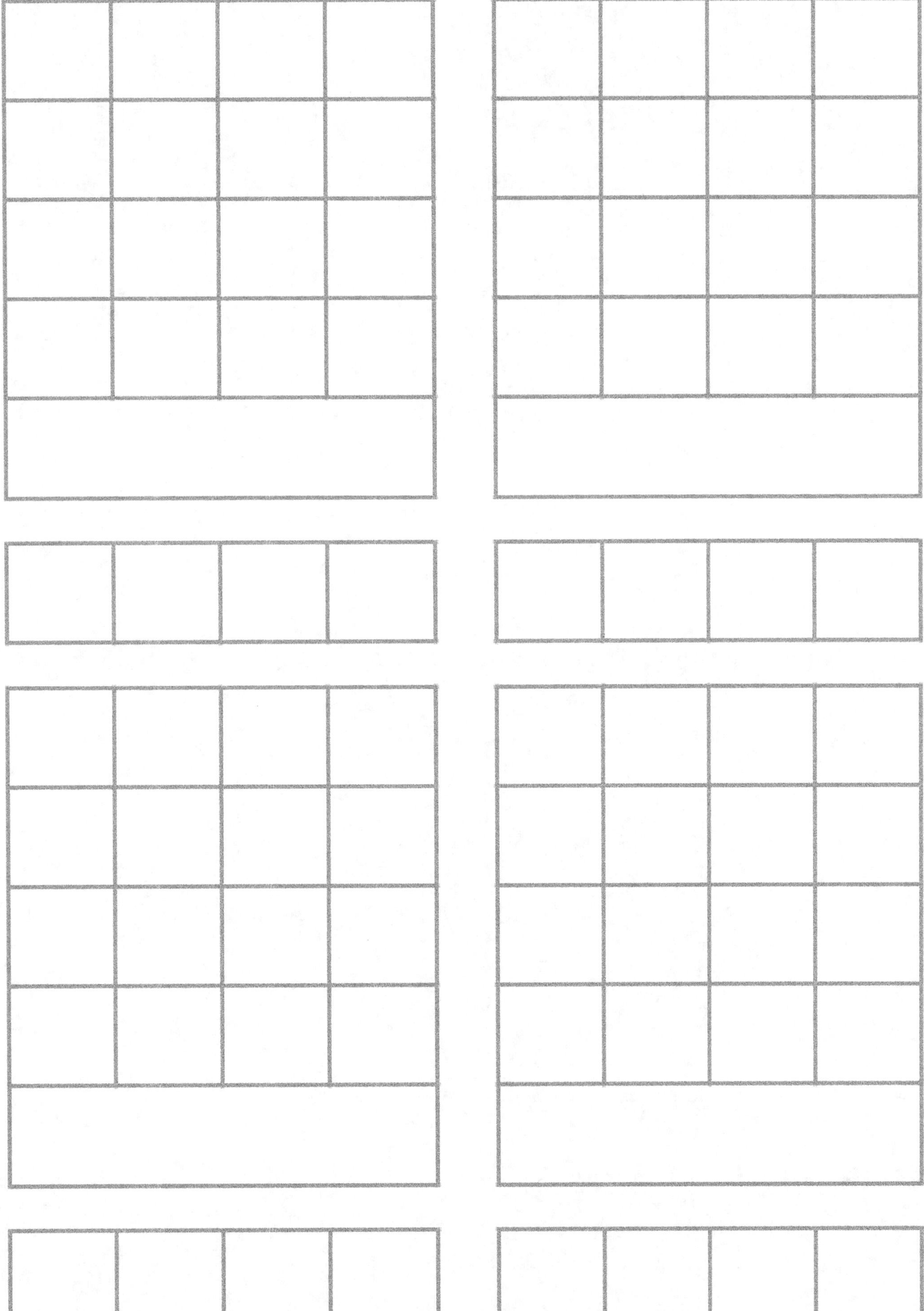

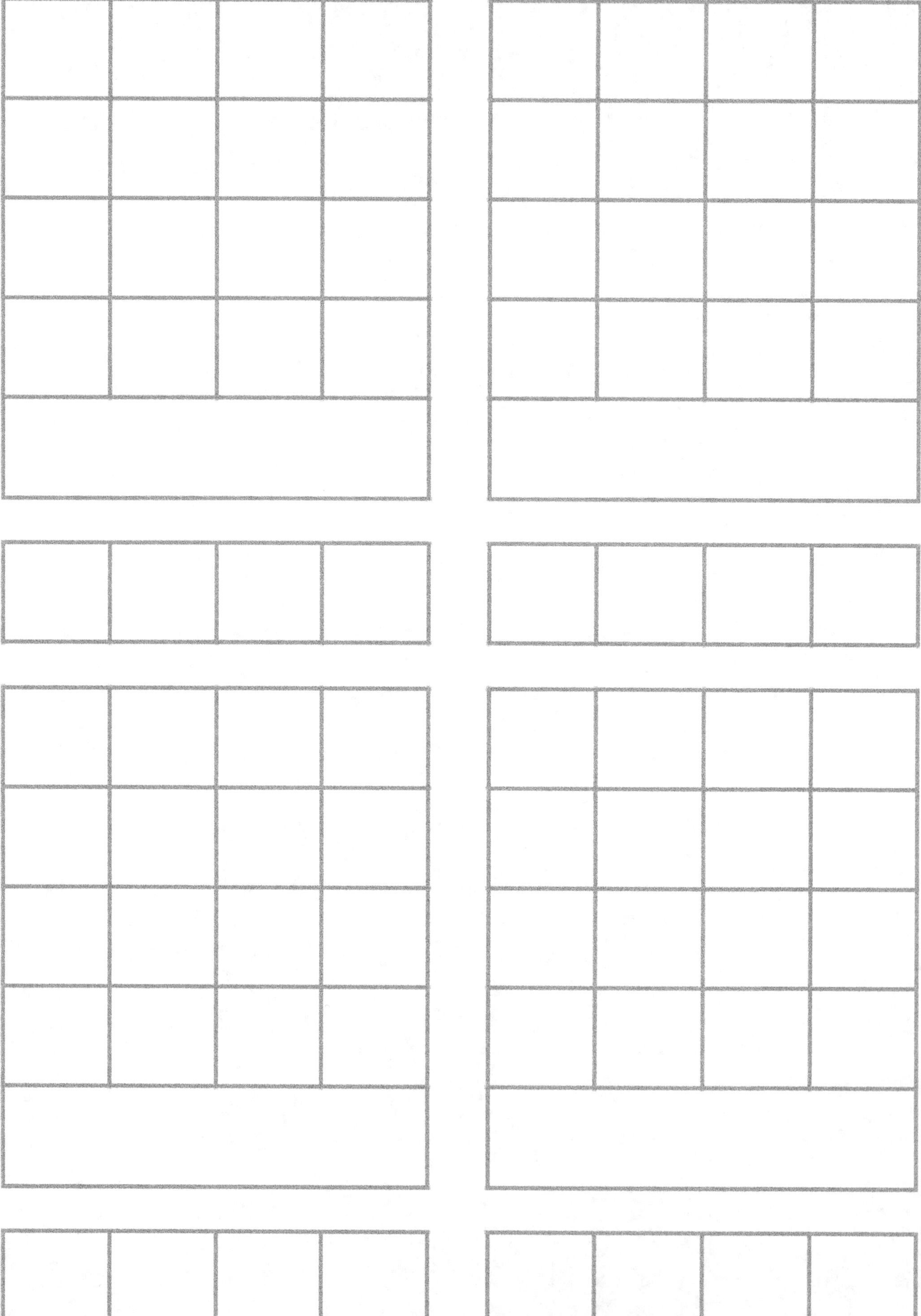

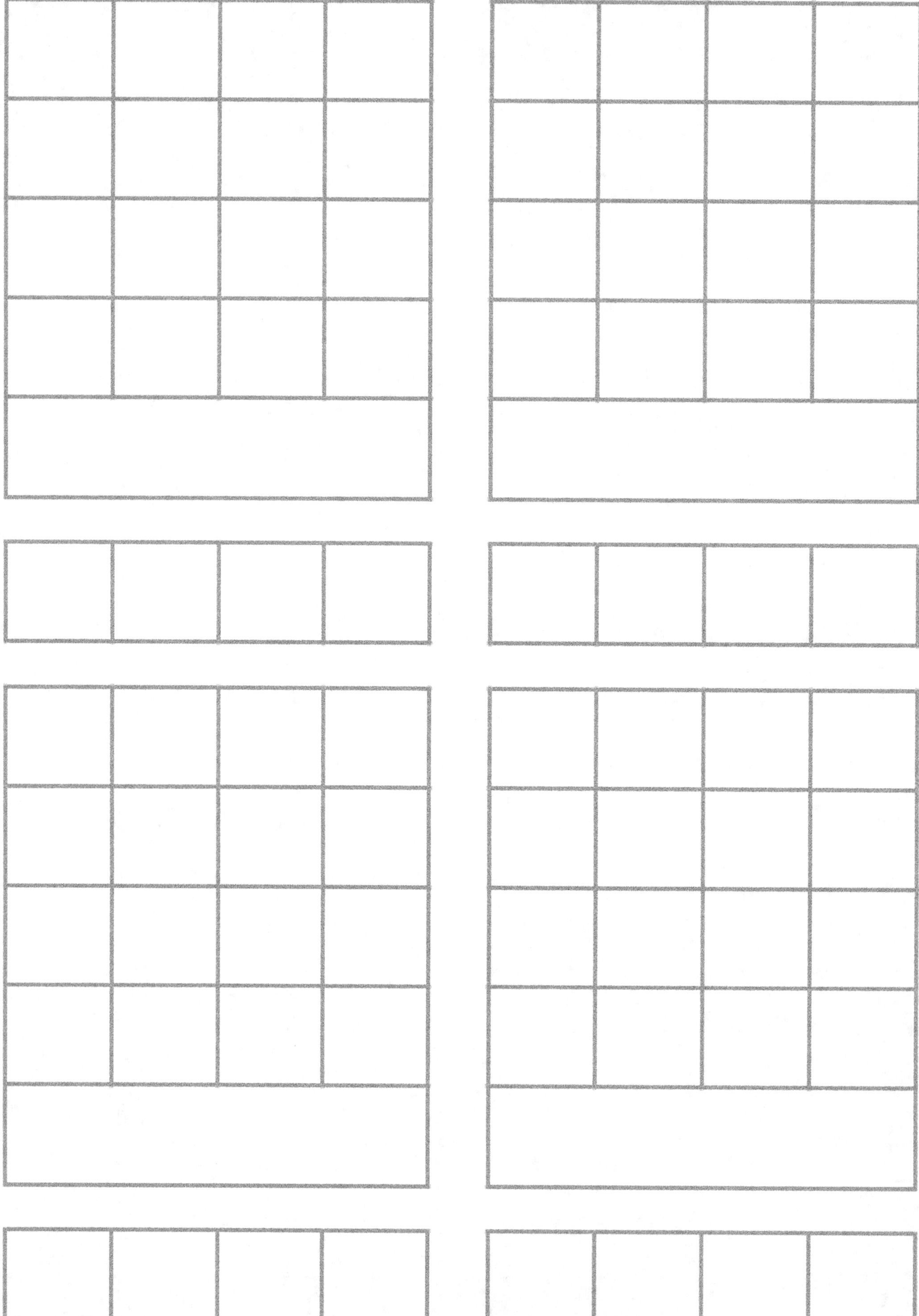

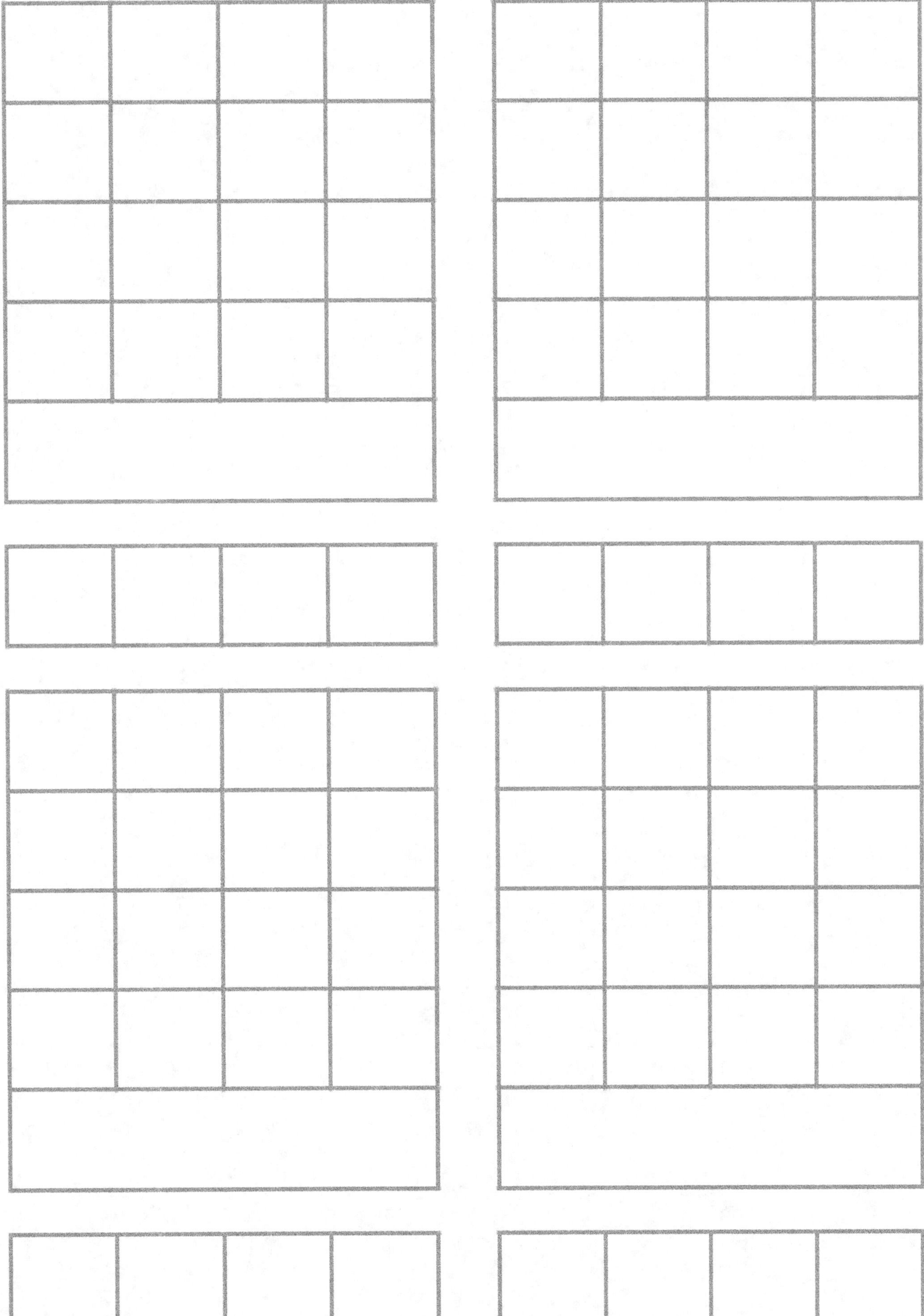

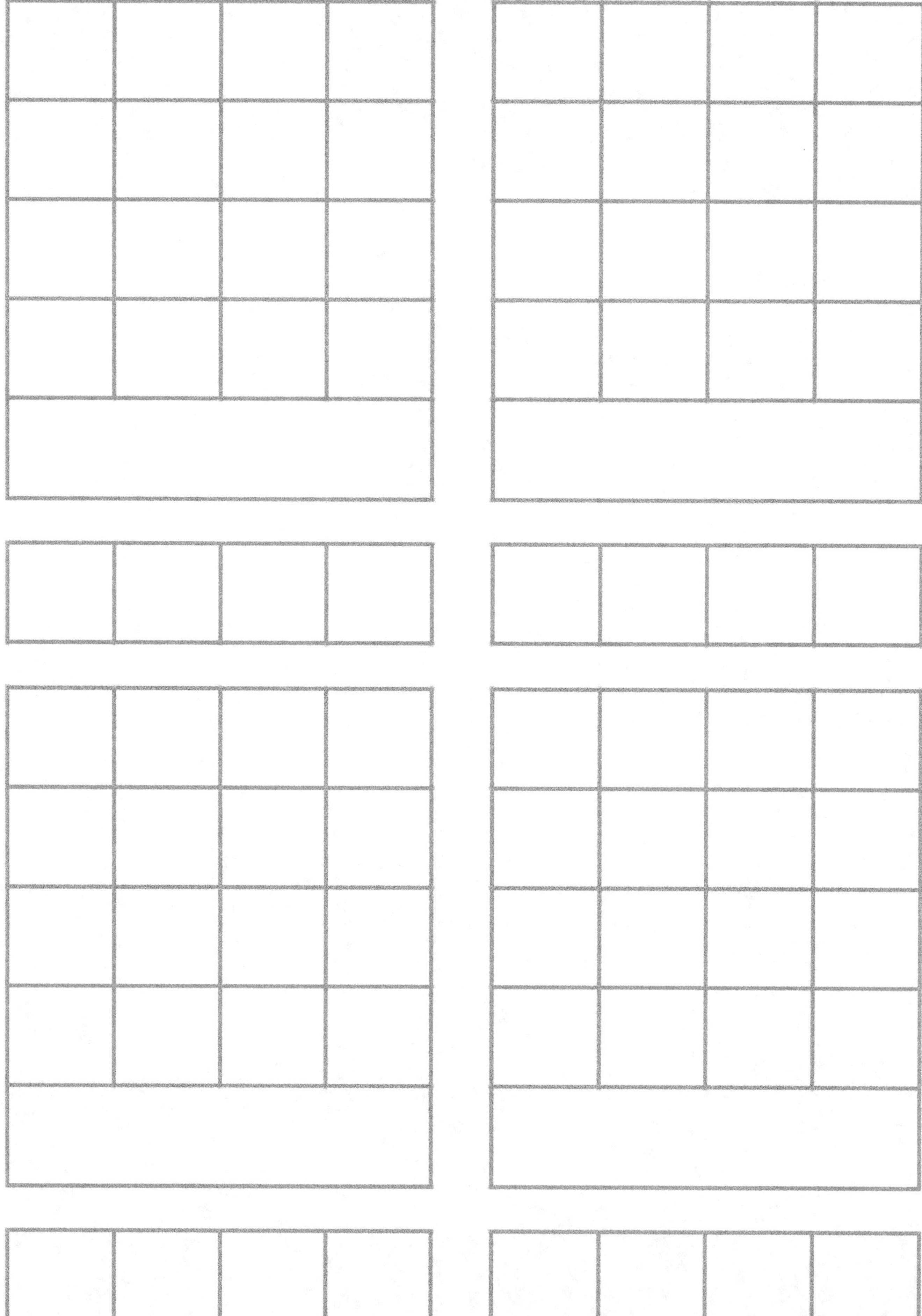

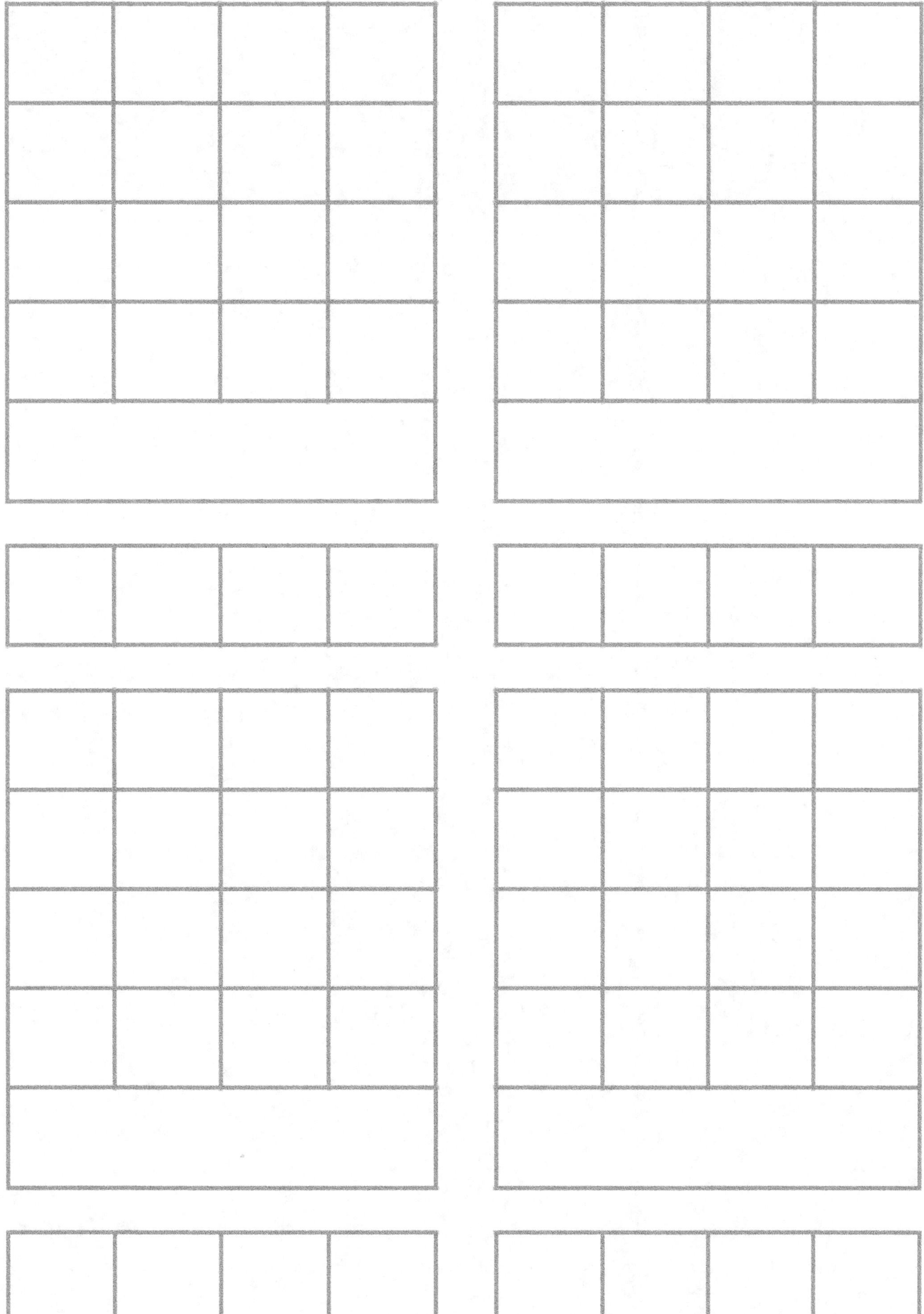

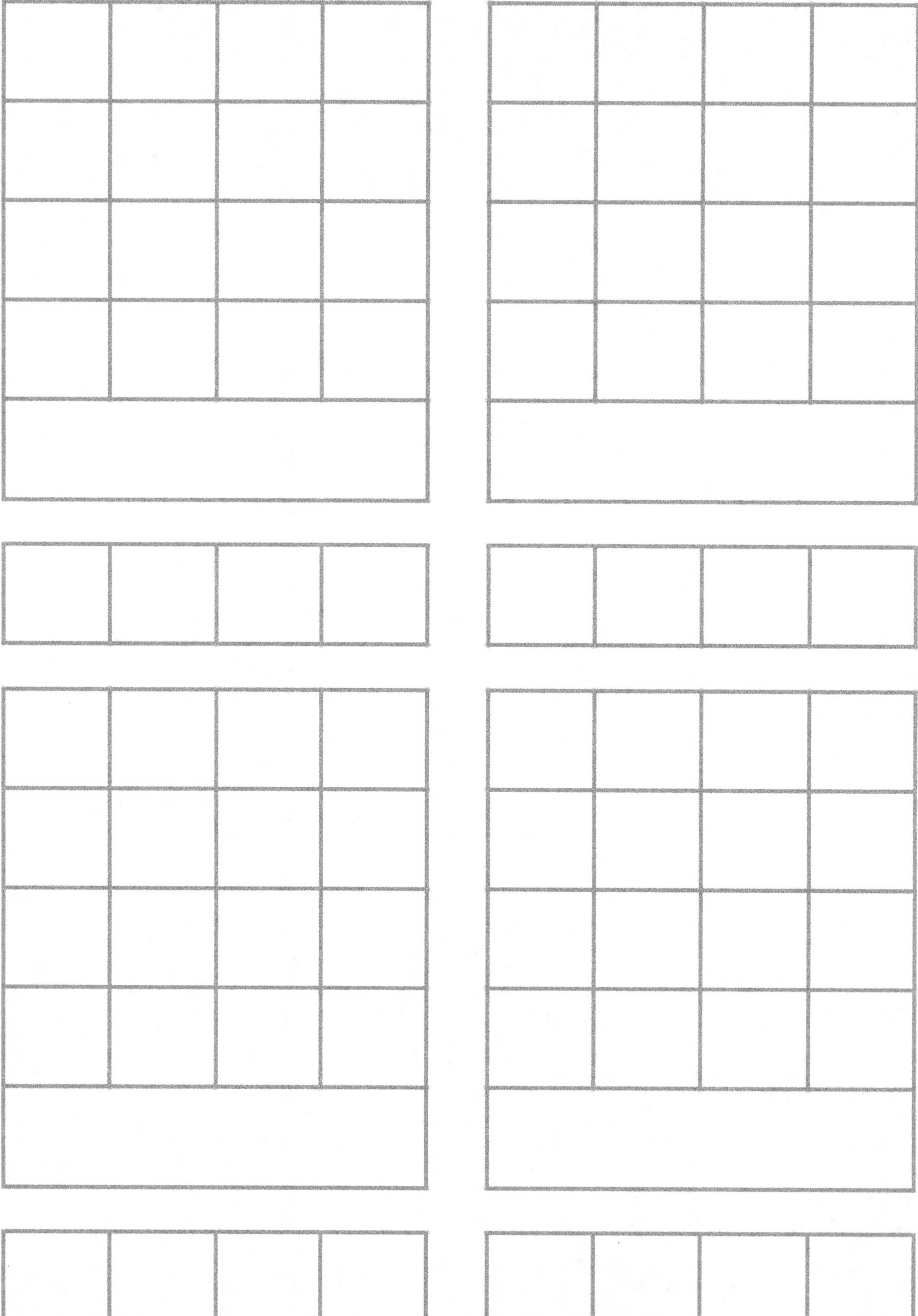

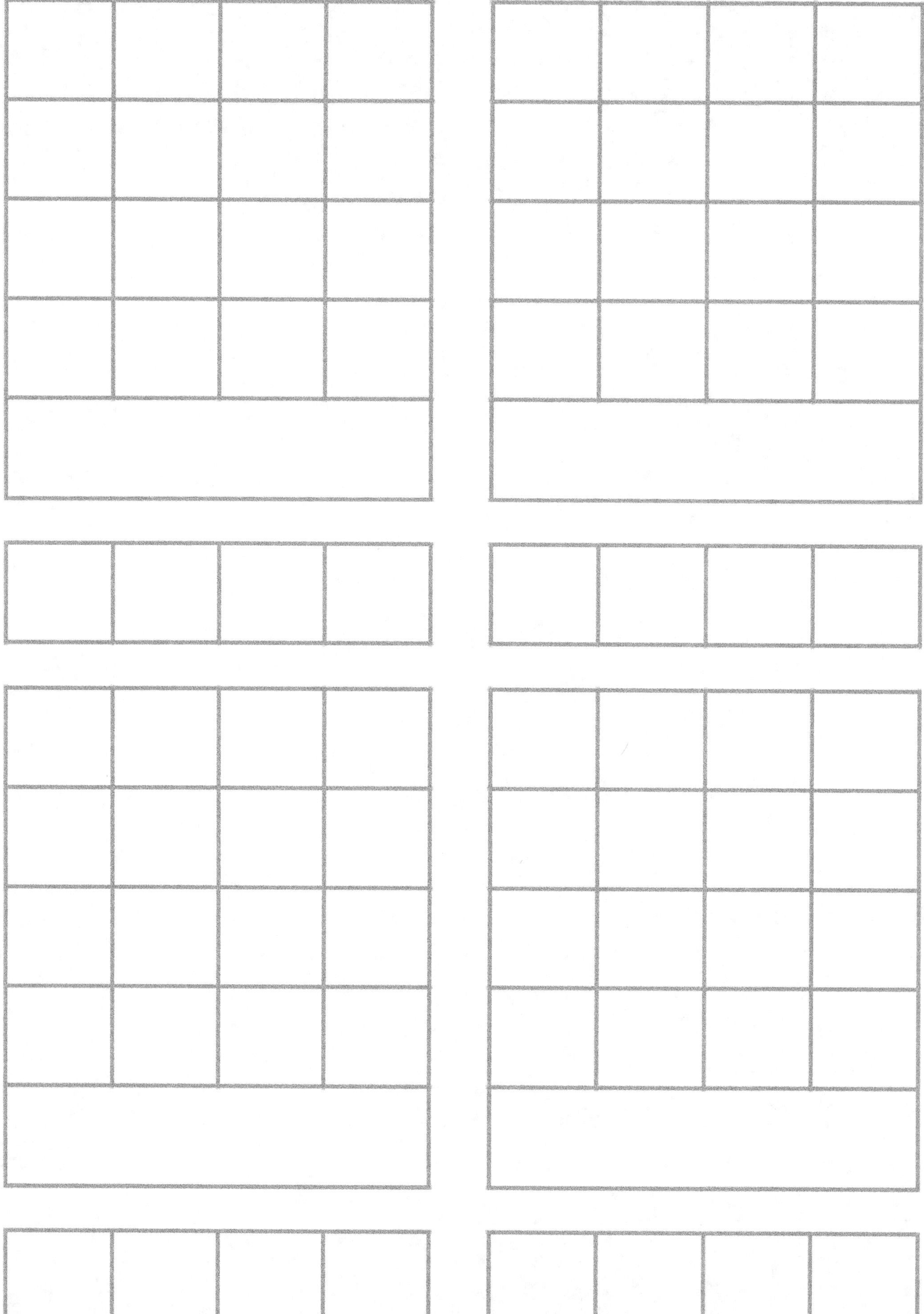

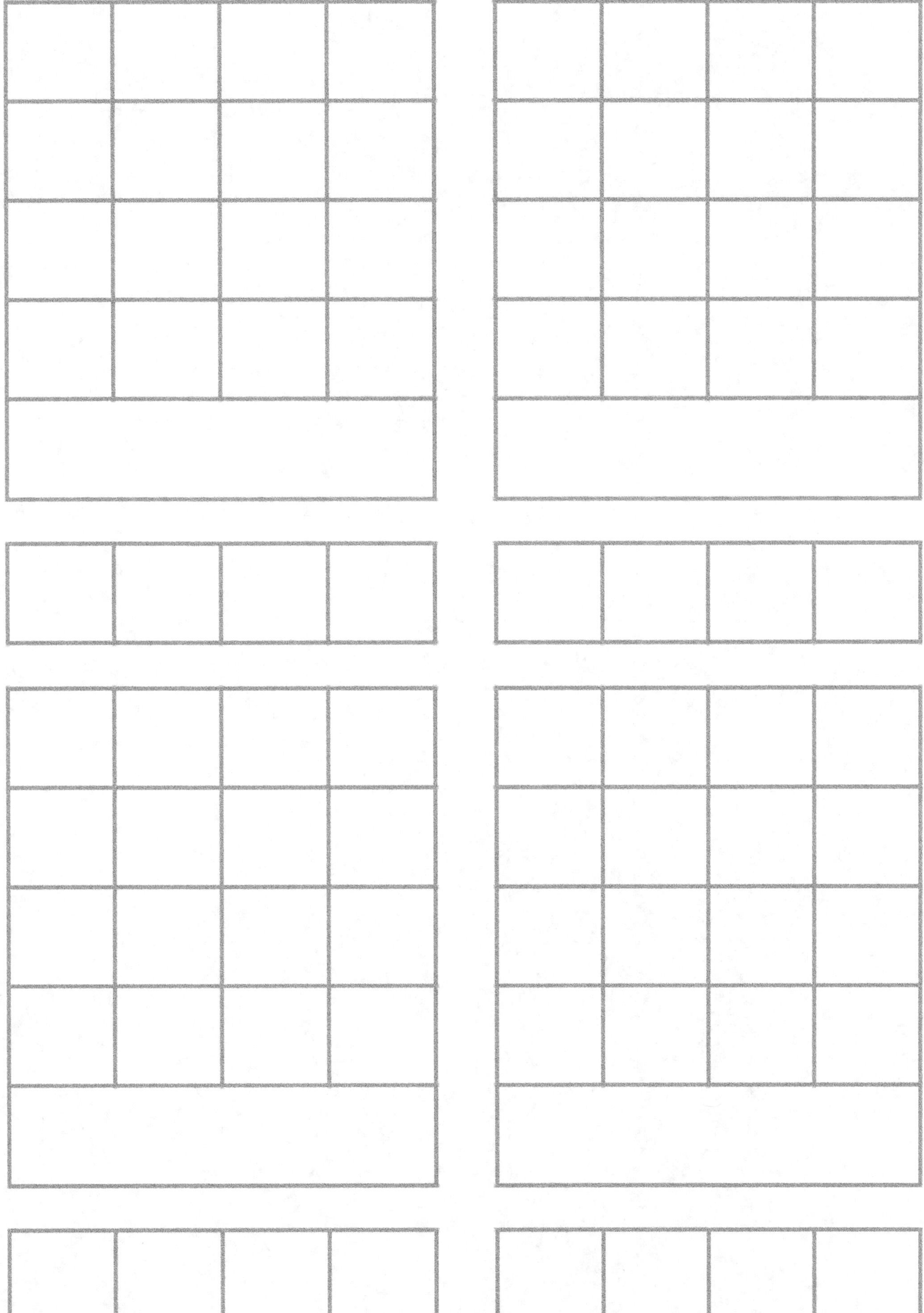

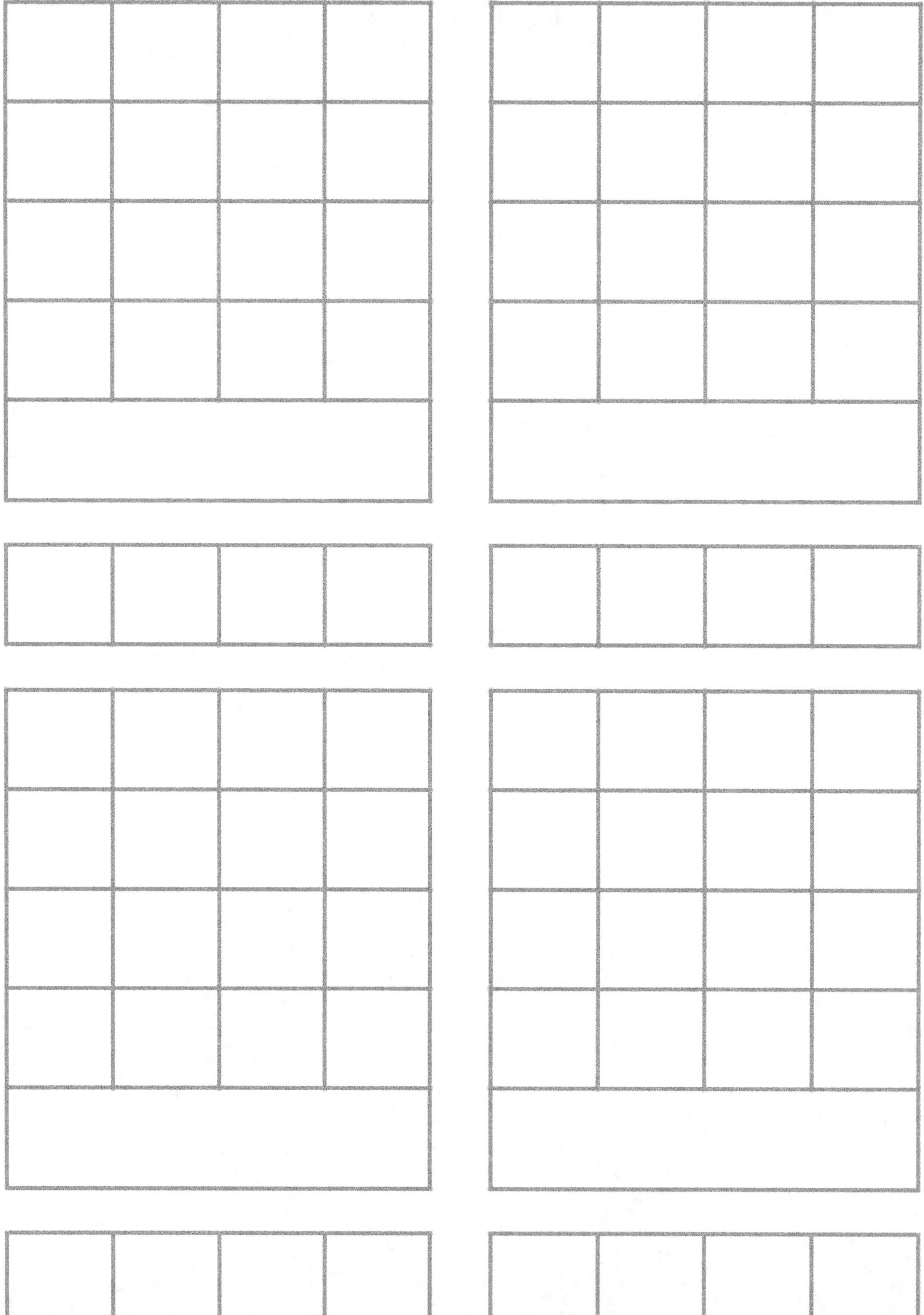

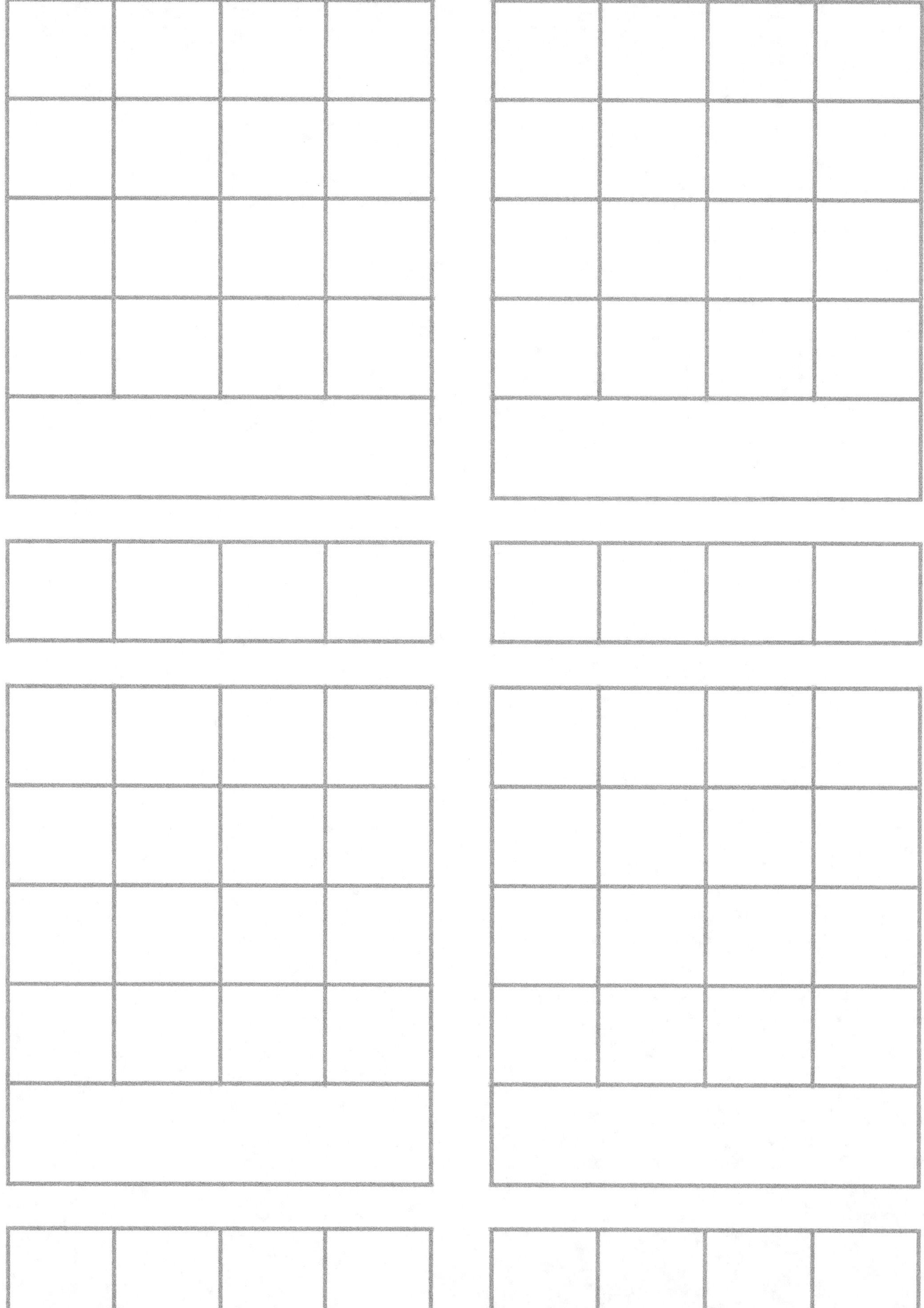

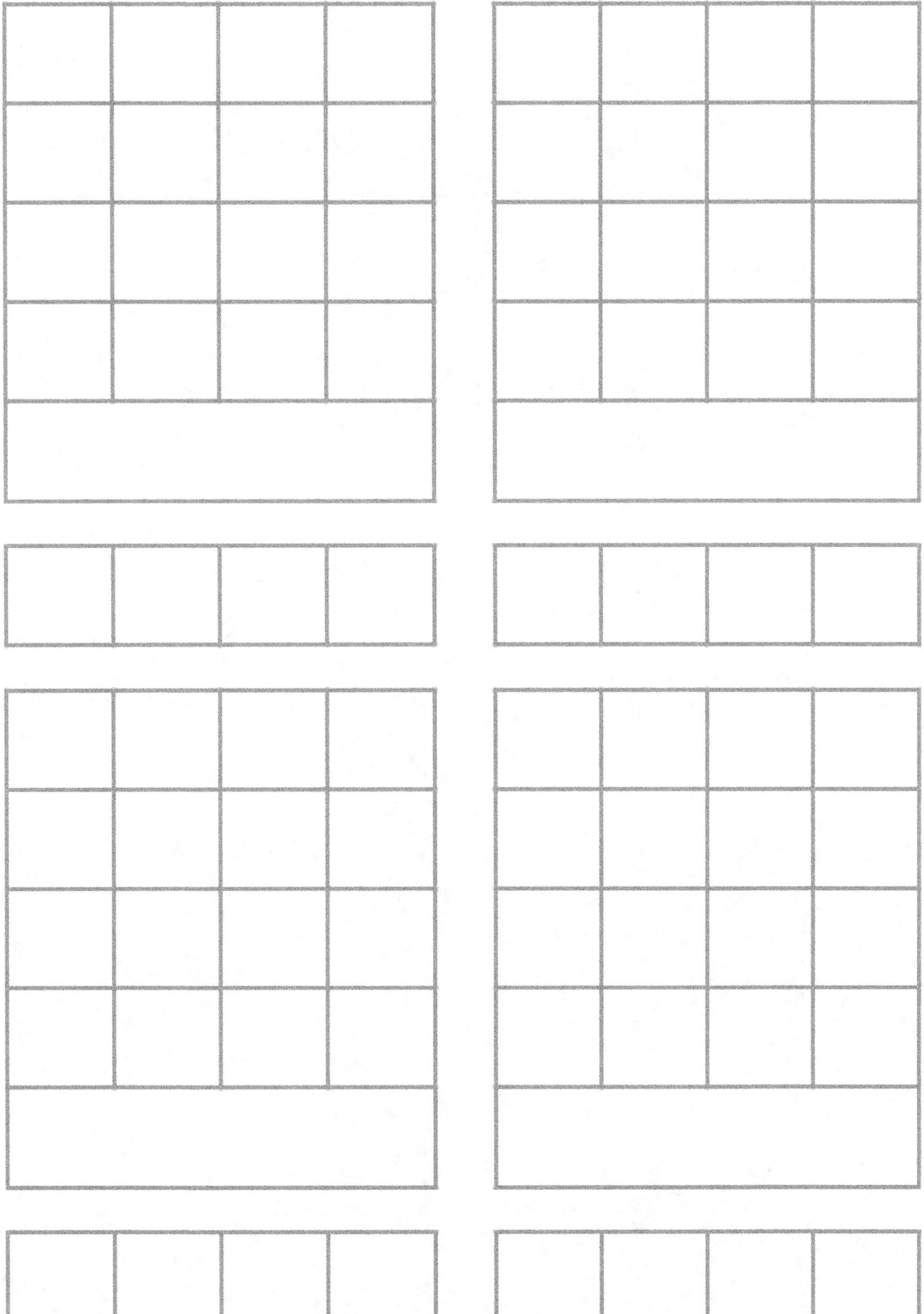

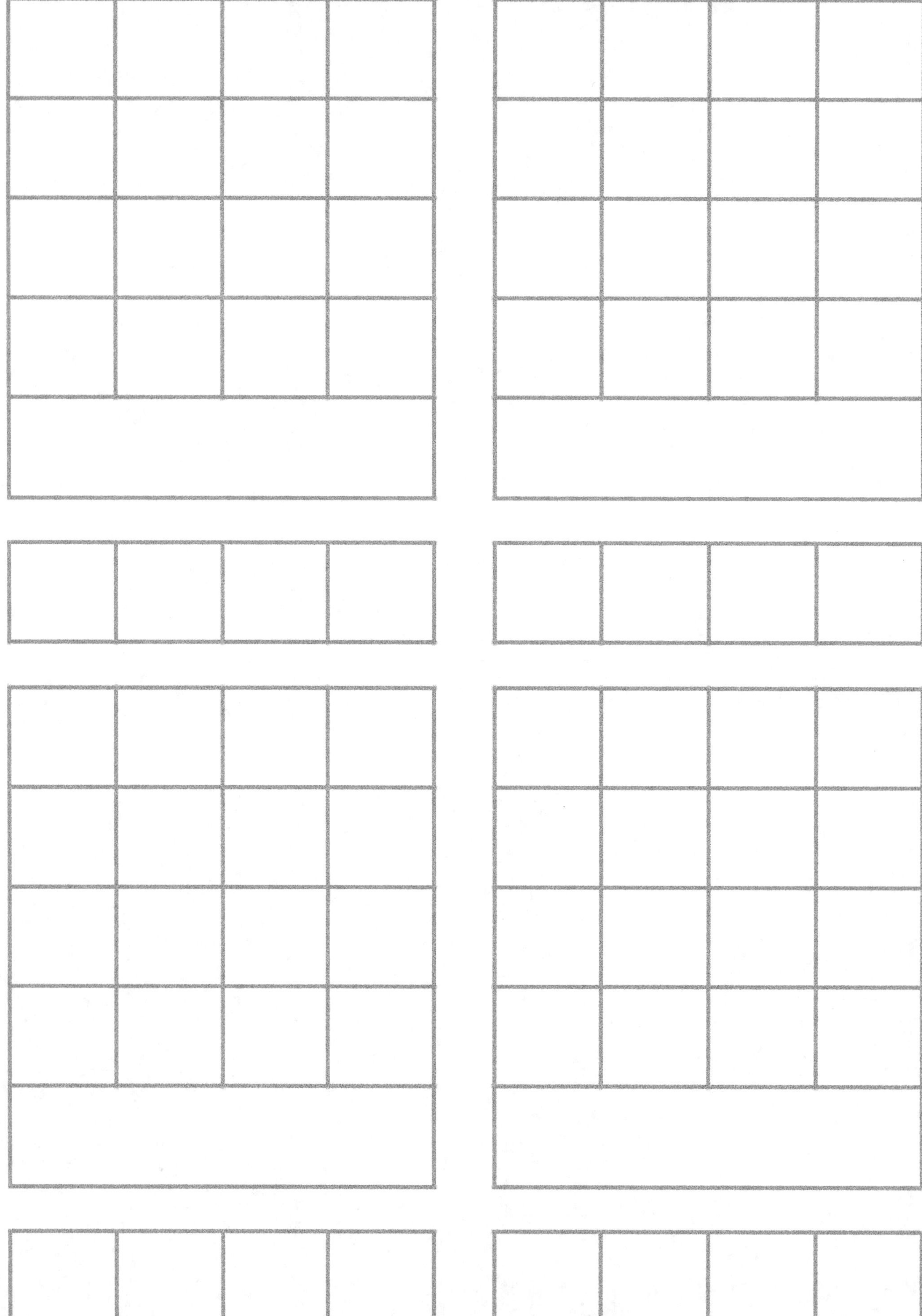

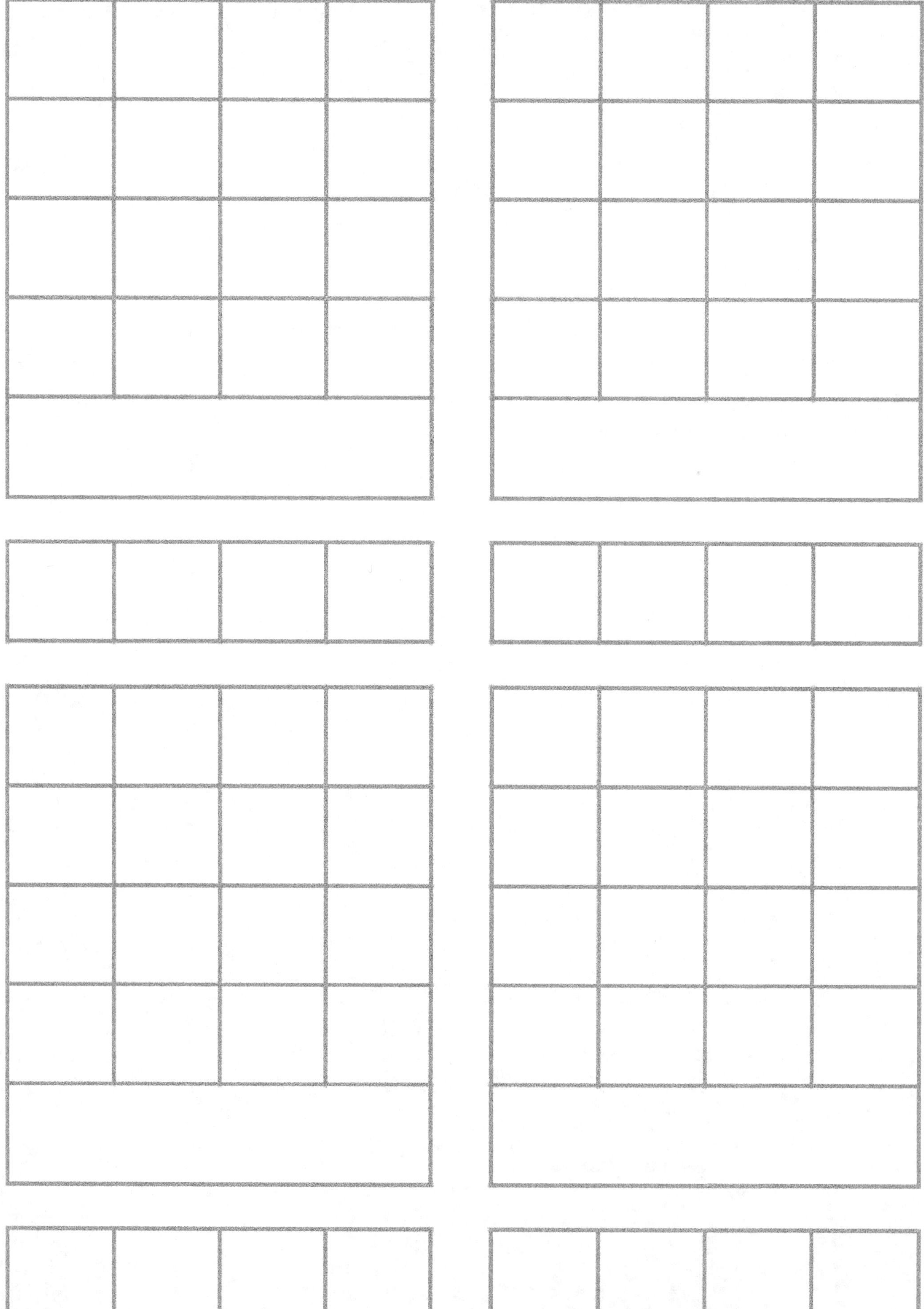

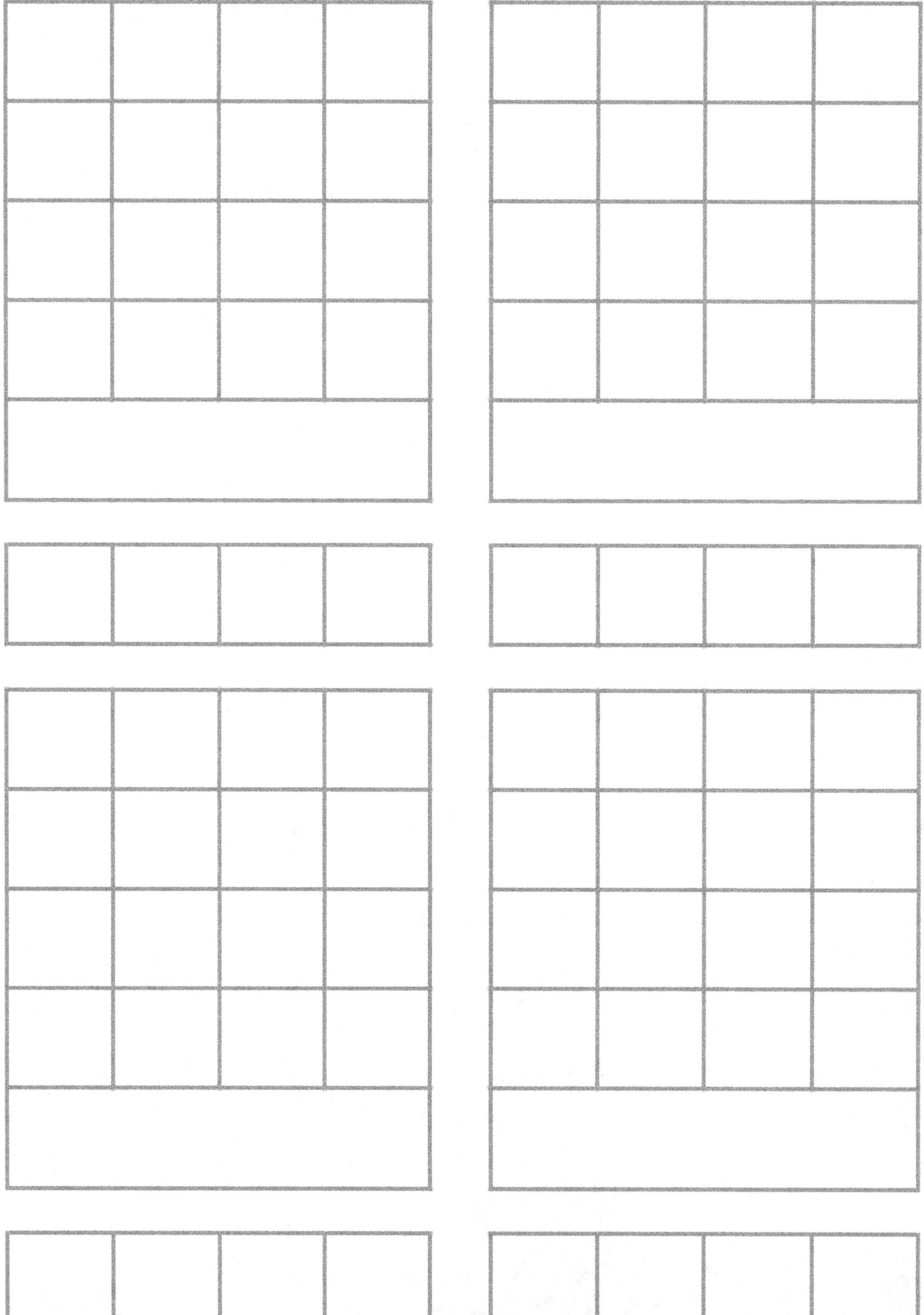

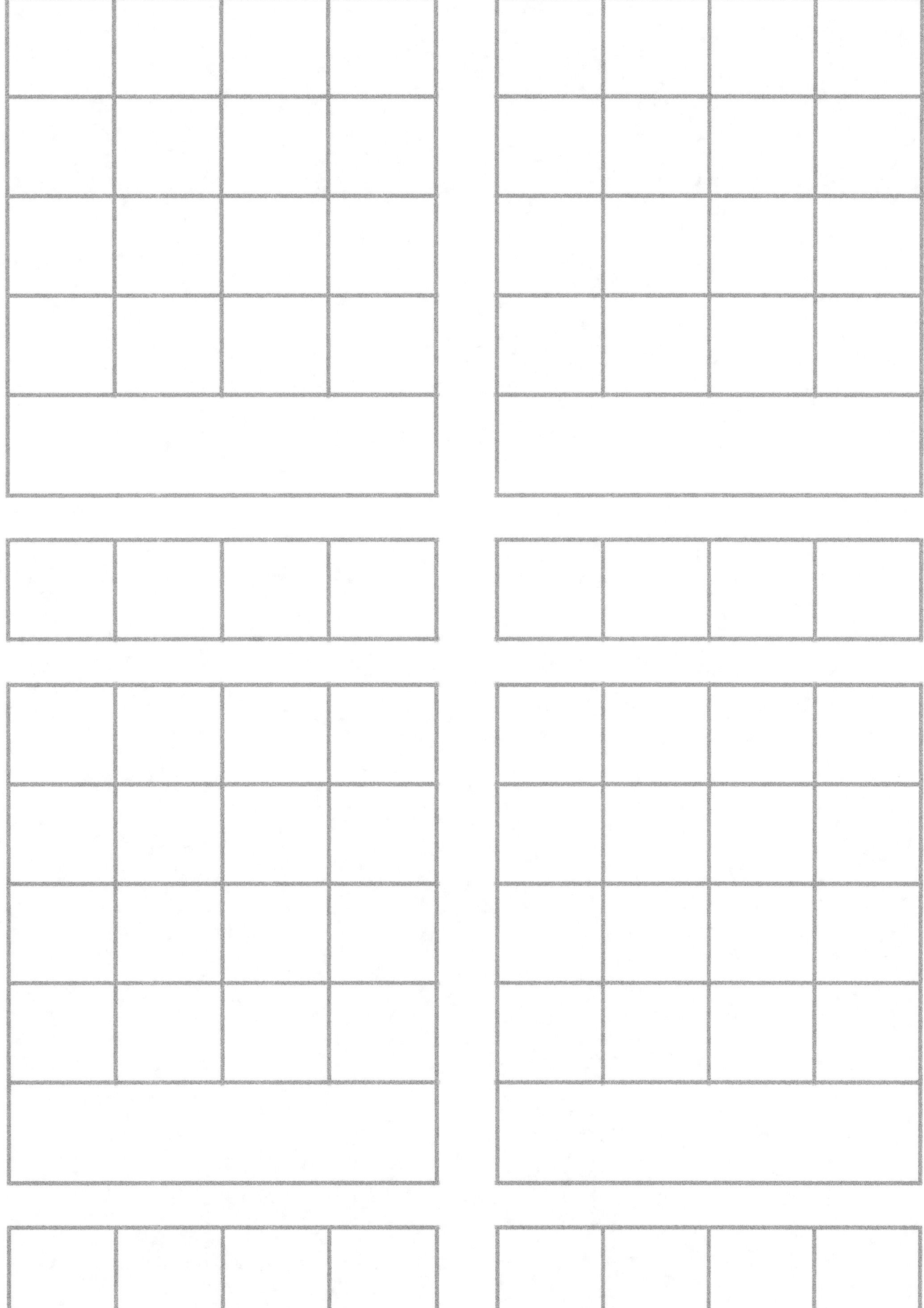

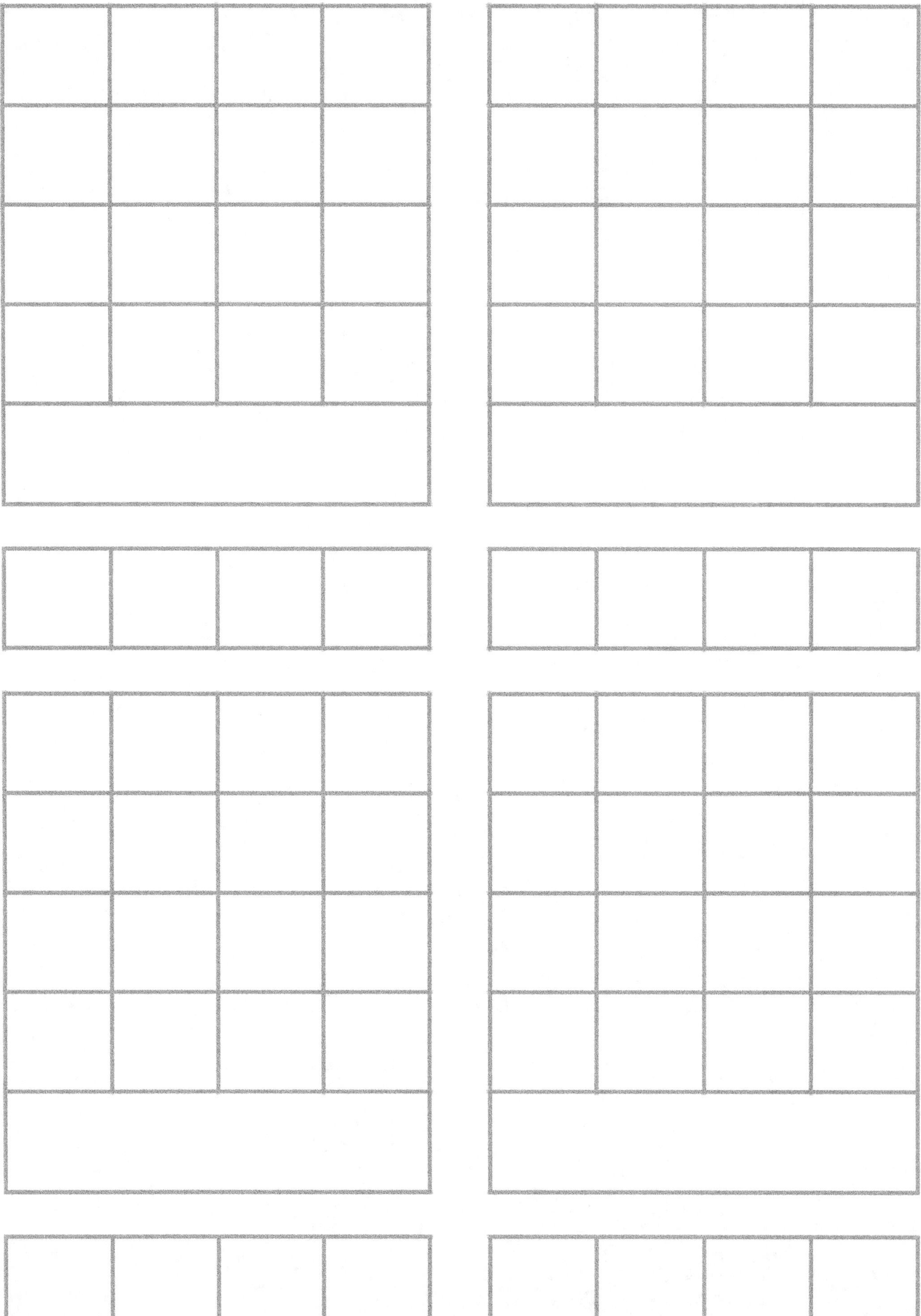

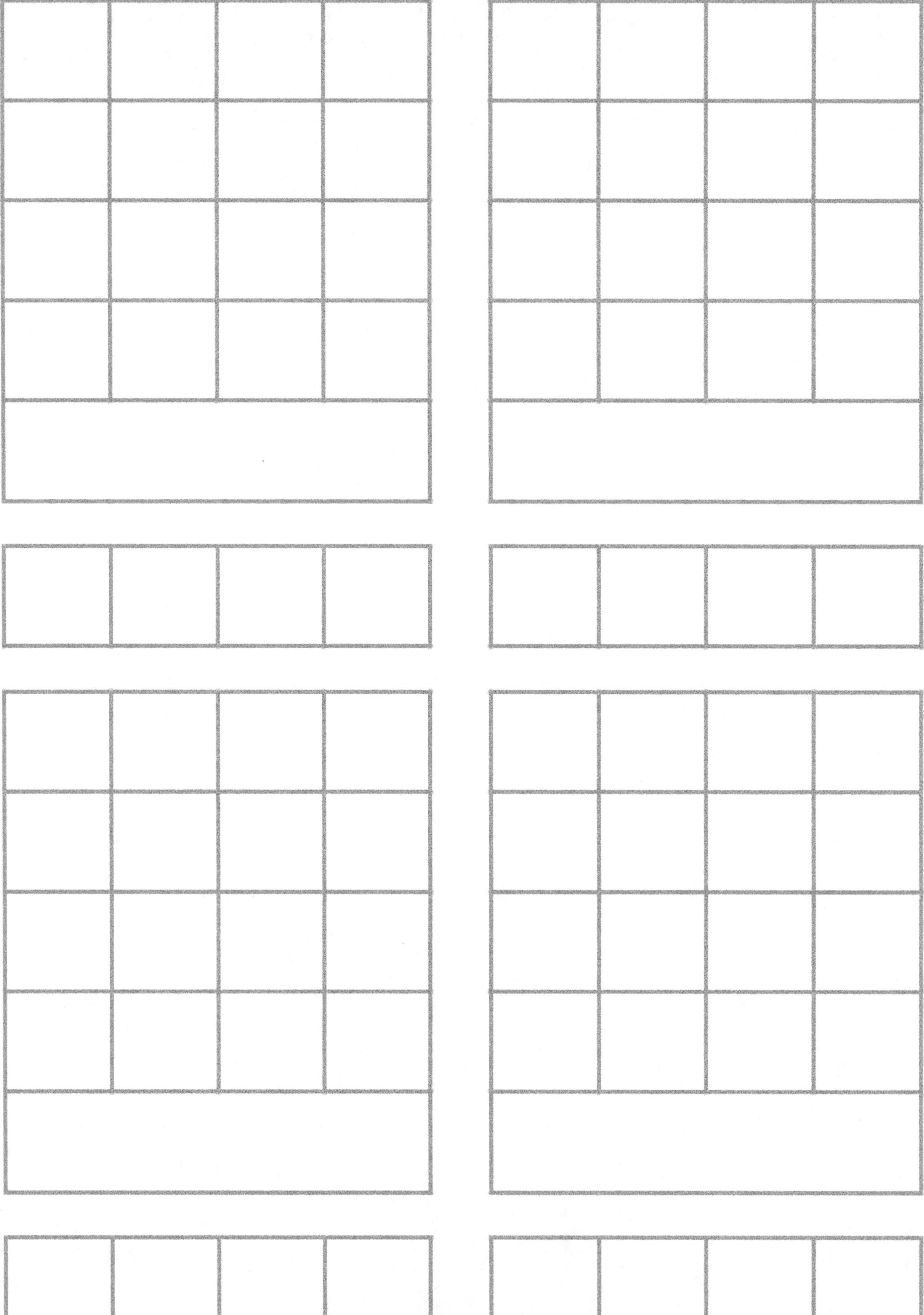

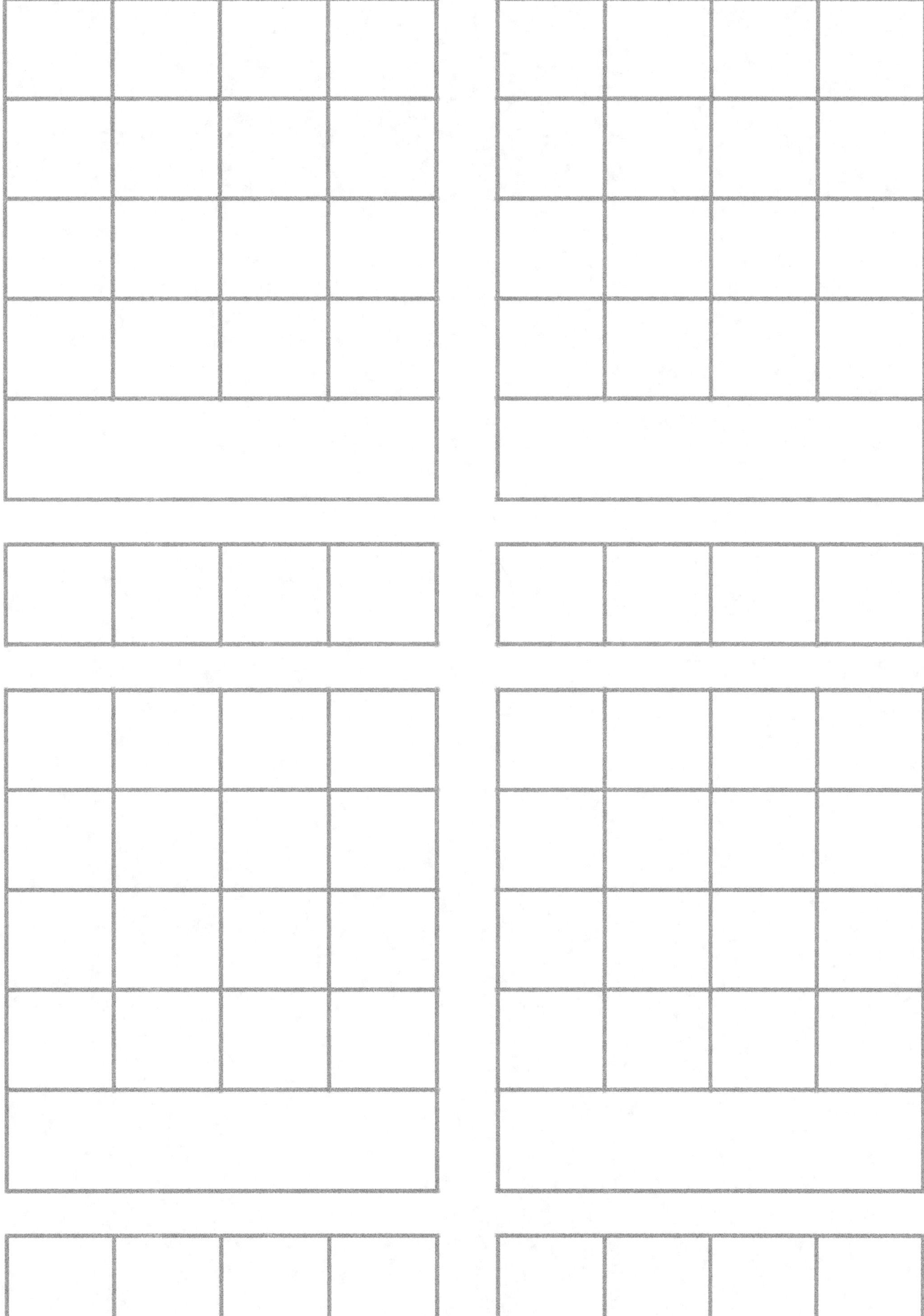

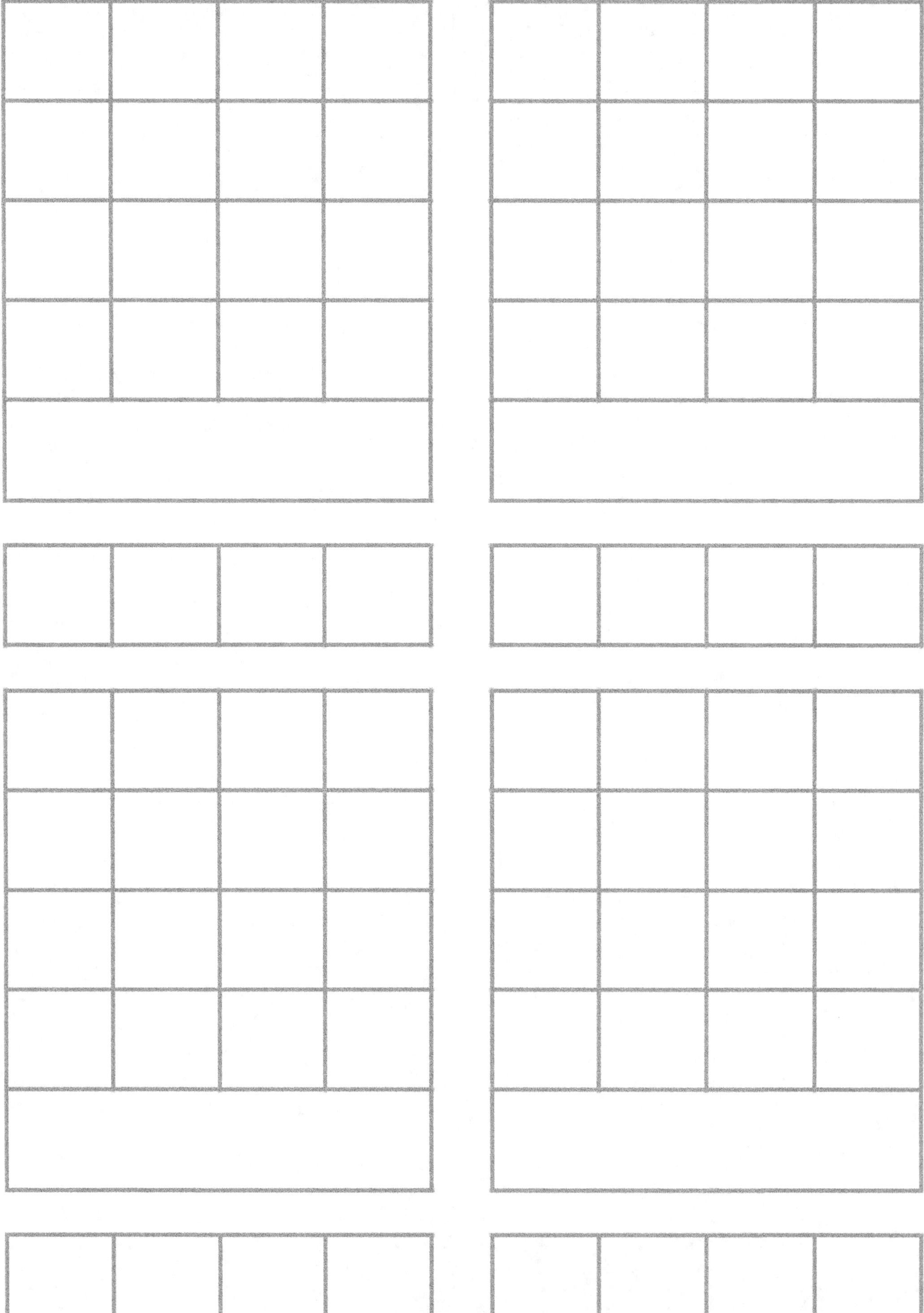

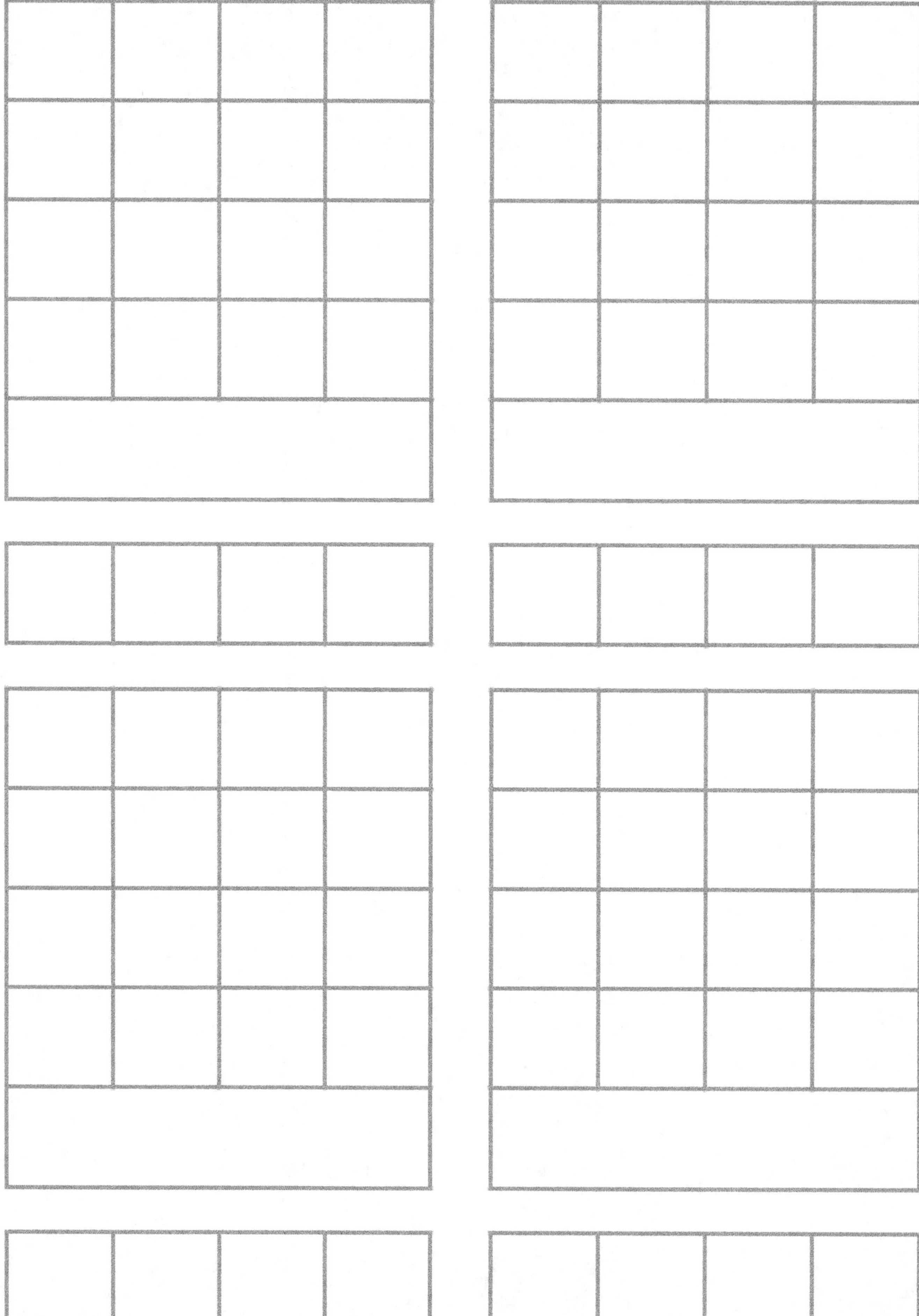

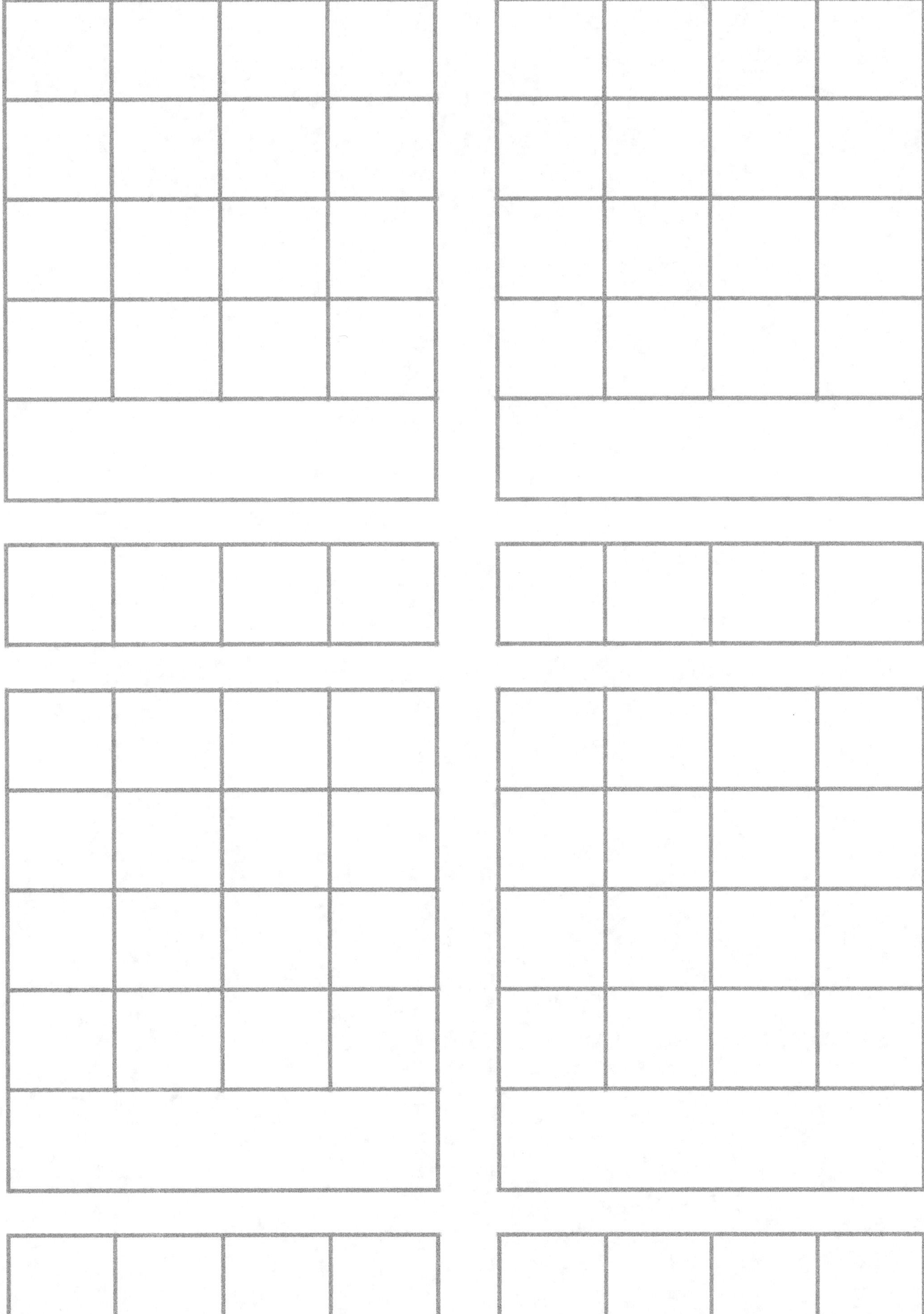

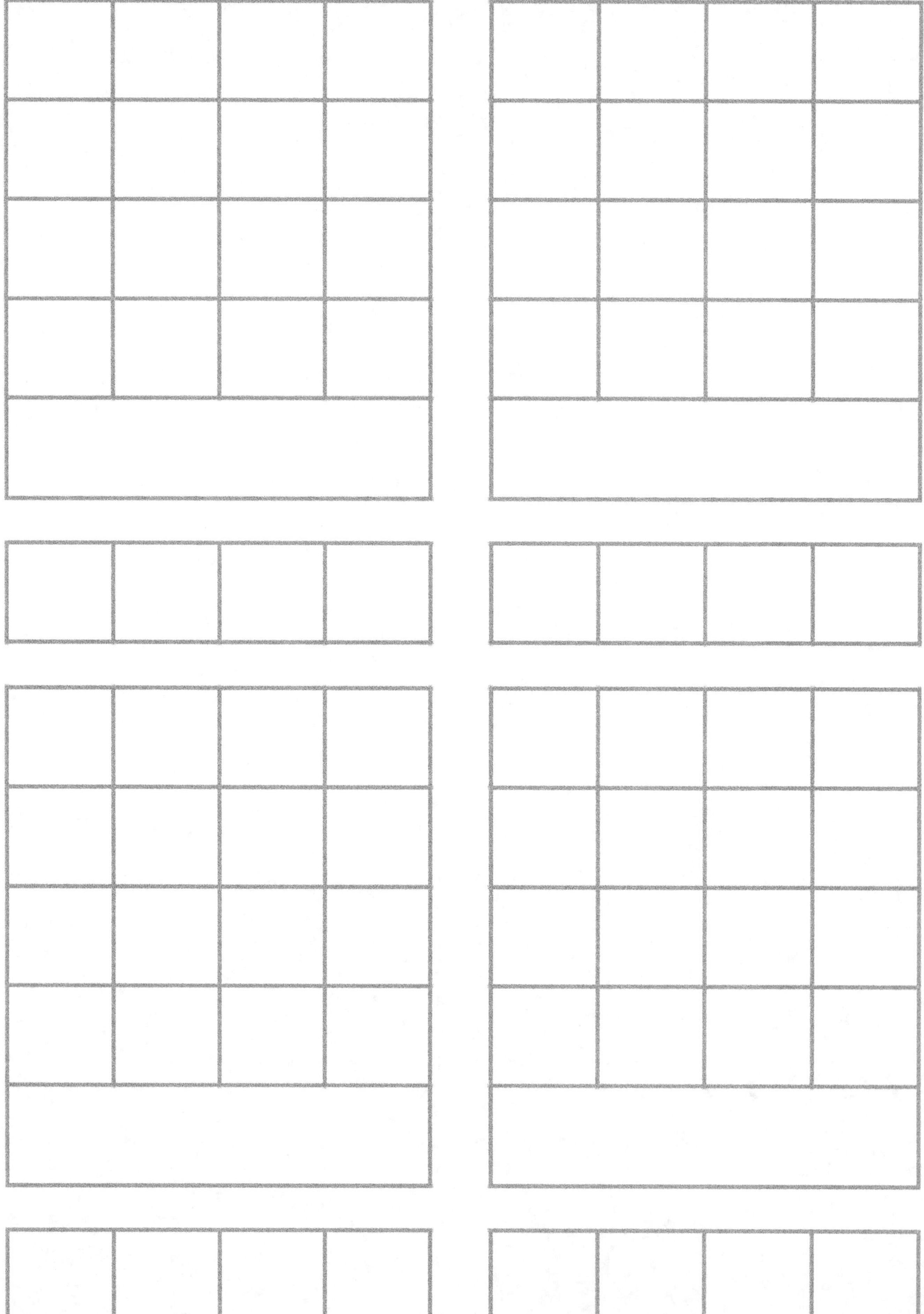

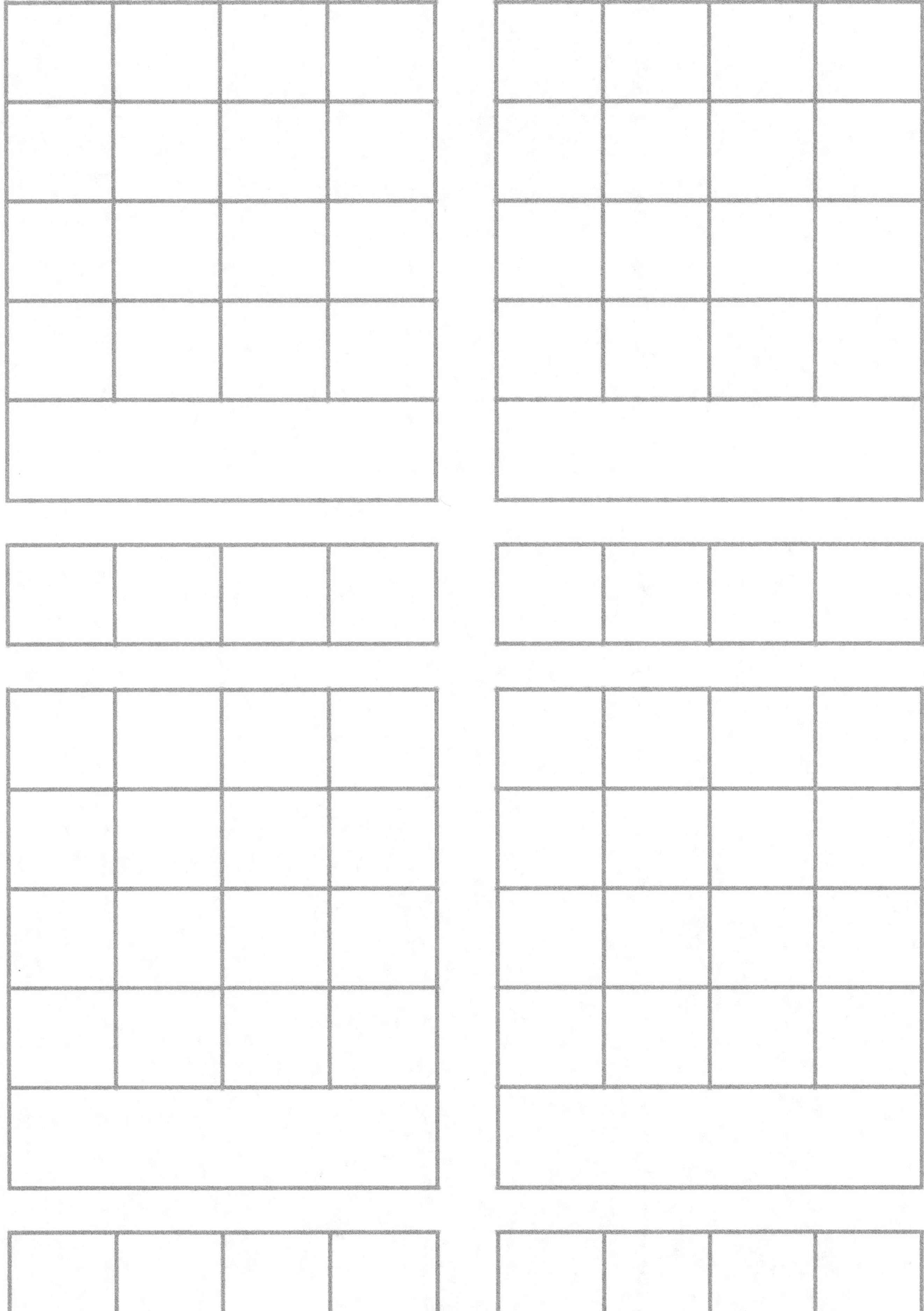

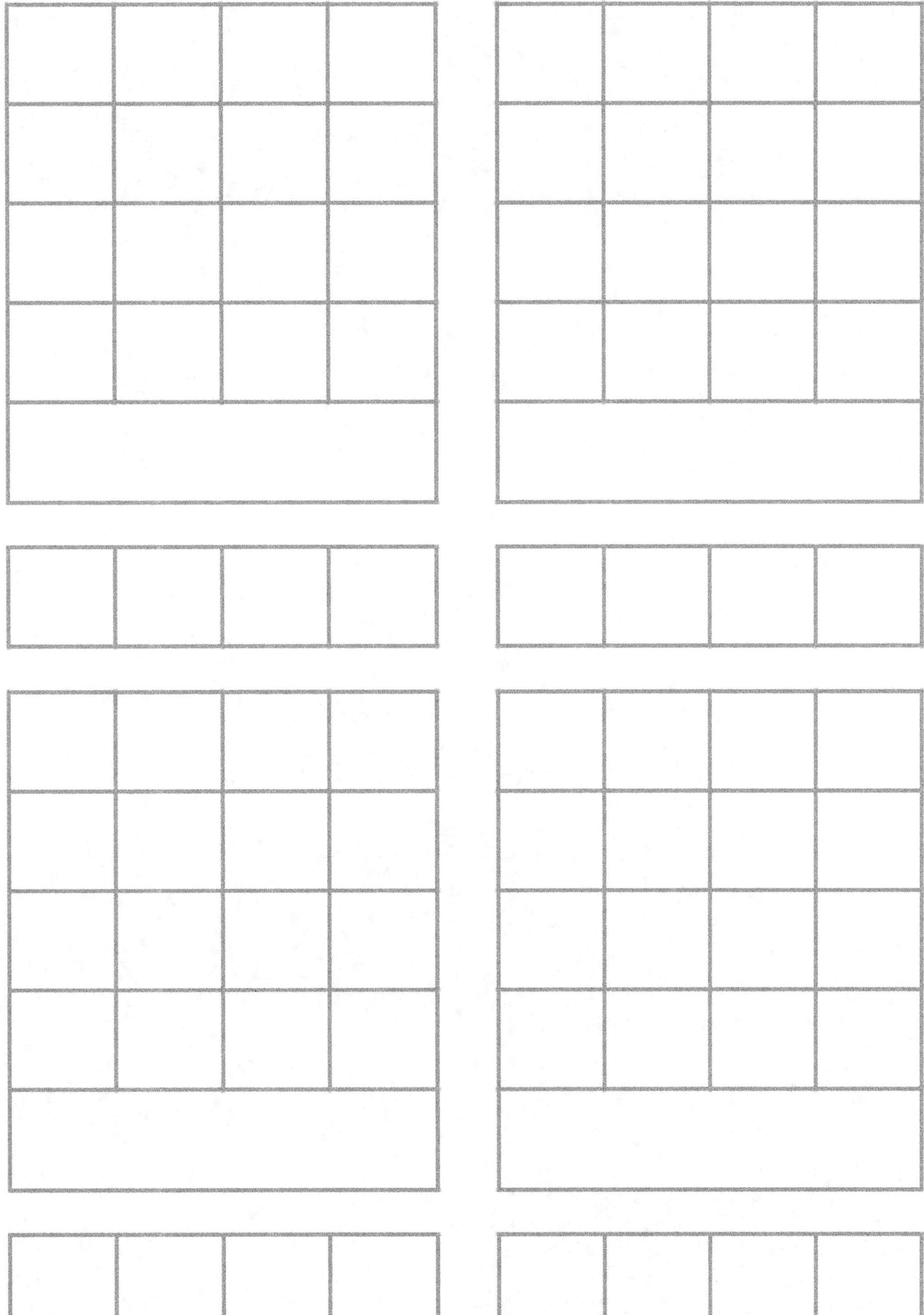

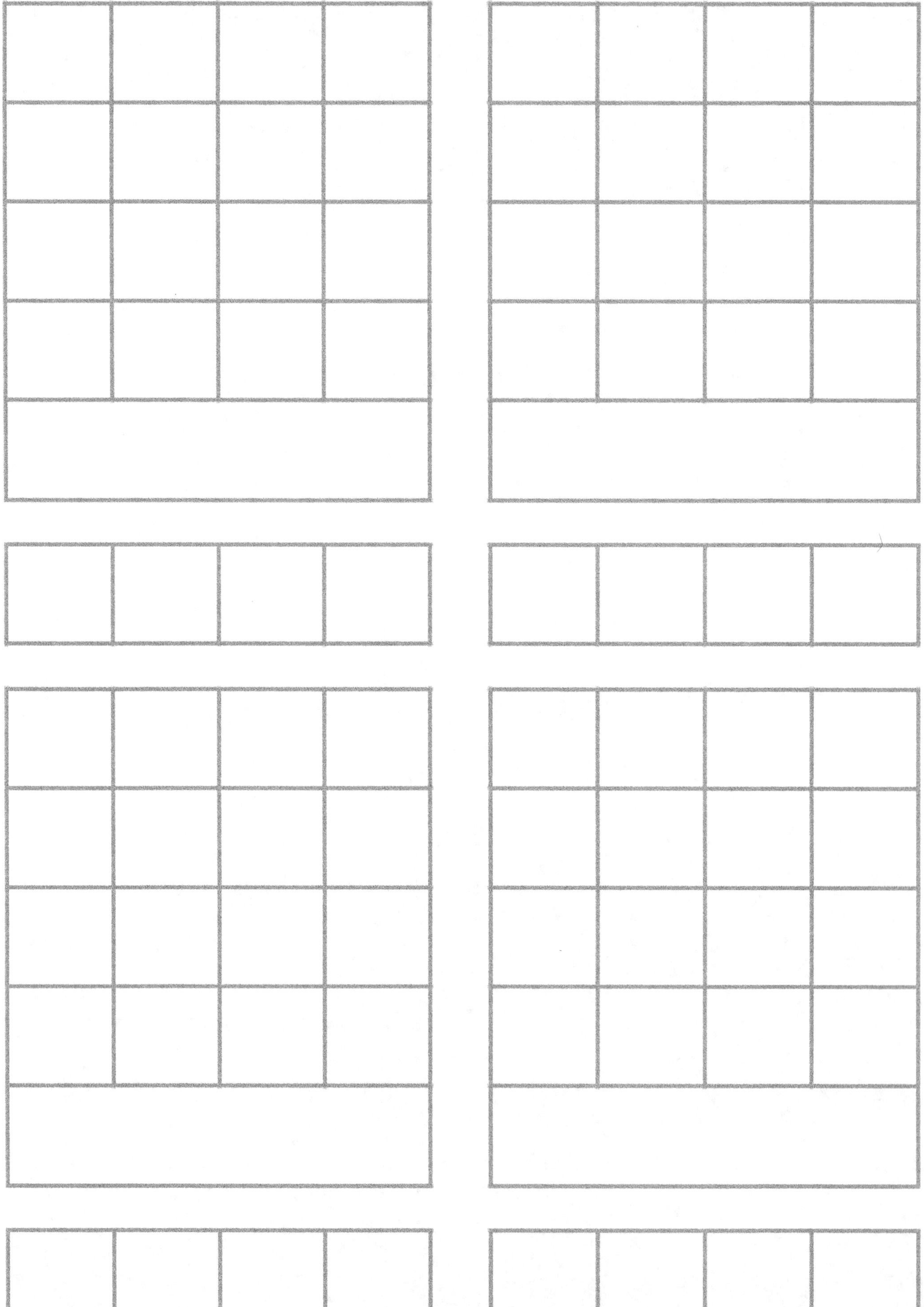

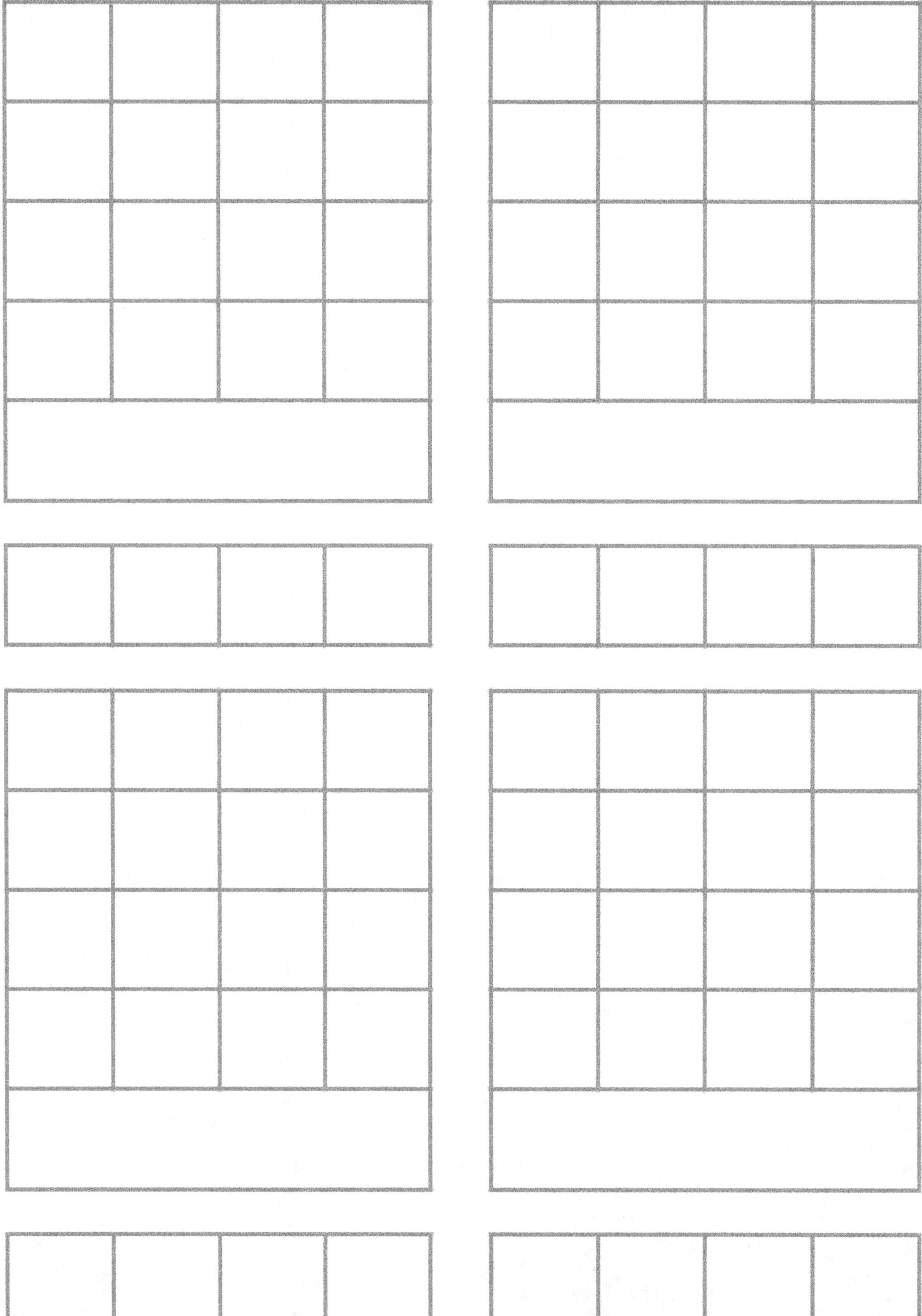

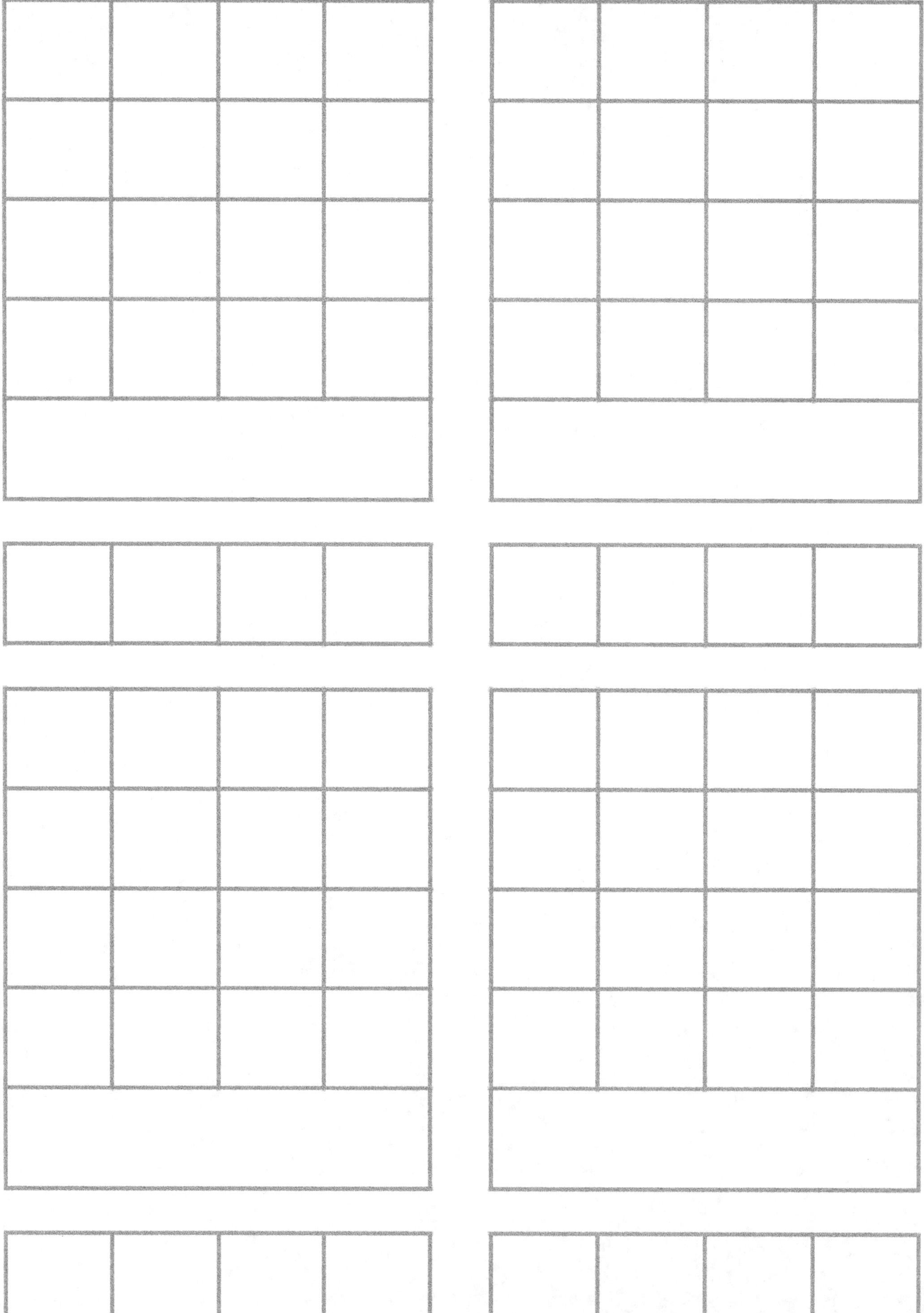